HOW TO GET DEBTS PAID FASTER

How to Get Debts Paid Faster

Roy Hedges

Gower

Published by
Gower Publishing Company Limited,
Gower House,
Croft Road,
Aldershot
Hants GU11 3HR,
England

British Library Cataloguing in Publication Data
Hedges, Roy
How to get debts paid faster.
1. Business firms. Credit management.–
Manuals.
I. Title.
658.8'8

ISBN 0 566 02787 9

Printed and bound in Great Britain at
The Camelot Press Ltd. Southampton

Contents

Foreword

There is no function in business more important than collecting and controlling the money that is owed. In this brief but eminently practical book Roy Hedges explains how the whole process of debt collection can be improved and accelerated.

I commend his ideas wholeheartedly to everyone concerned with credit control.

Sir Anthony Jolliffe, GBE, FCA
Chairman
Walker Greenbank Plc

Preface

This book is designed to turn your credit control and cash collection into a *positive* process, rather than the *negative* one it still is in many companies.

All too often, credit control departments are used as a last resort. They are brought in when all else fails, using shock-trooper tactics to cow the company's enemies into submission. A single threatening, hostile telephone call from a credit controller can undo months or years of good work by the rest of your company in fostering good relations with a customer. And if customers start taking their business elsewhere because you are being insensitive in collecting the money they owe you, your credit controllers are losing you more money than they are bringing in.

Your credit control department should be an efficient link in the chain of selling products and collecting money for them. This means that the emphasis should be on managing and collecting debts *before* they become overdue, not after. Credit control is a *service* to your customers, not a weapon to be used against them.

Cash is one of the most important assets of any business. But, in many cases, the vital task of managing this asset has been placed in the hands of low-paid, untrained staff who have simply been given a printout of the company's sales ledger with the debts listed by age, and told to get on with the job. The ideas presented in this book stem from my work as a consultant specializing in cash control for more than a decade. During that time I have created credit control systems for companies of every size from small to multinational. The results have included permanently reduced sales ledger debt and better relationships with customers.

Not all of this book will be relevant to every reader; possibly there are whole chapters which you will not be able to apply. And, while the book describes methods relating mainly to the larger company which employs full-time credit managers and/or controllers, the philosophy behind these methods is the same whatever the size of the company. You do not need droves of people on the telephone eight hours a day to get your cash working for you more effectively.

Roy Hedges

1 What your credit controllers should be doing for you

Arthur Beansprout is a good credit controller. He's been working for your company for longer than he cares to remember. He sits there all day in a cloud of cigarette smoke with the phone to his ear and a printout in front of him, and he knows the company, its products and his clients inside out. The good thing about him is that he can introduce just the right air of menace into his voice to suit the age of the debt. On the back of your company's invoices, there is a little note in the bottom right-hand corner that says: 'Terms of trade strictly one month nett'. Nobody is quite sure what the word 'nett' means in this case, but it's always said that, so why change it?

So, when two months have gone by and Trimmett and Co. still have not paid one of their invoices, he is on the phone to them, first thing on Monday morning. He speaks to Mrs Platt, his opposite number in Trimmett and Co's bought ledger department.

'Morning, Mrs Platt,' he says. His gruffness is calculated, and borne of years of practice. He hasn't got time to waste on pleasantries. 'Don't seem to have had the money for invoice no. 22538'. £15.78, you owe us. What's the problem?'

Mrs Platt doesn't know, but she says she will speak to her manager and call him back. Later on, she does.

'I'm sorry about that invoice of yours, Mr Beansprout', she says. 'But my manager says apparently we ordered a case of stainless steel eyebolts and you sent us ordinary steel ones by mistake. They're no use to us, so we asked your sales department to come and pick them up. That was a month ago, and they still haven't come, so my manager's put a stop on paying the invoice.'

Arthur grunts into the receiver by way of acknowledgement and puts the phone down. He writes a memo to the sales department to ask them to get a move on. Sometimes he makes a note on the sales ledger. Then he puts the annoying incident out of his mind and goes on to his next call.

A month later, the name of Trimmett and Co. appears on his printout again. This time, it's not just the invoice for £15.78, which is now two months overdue, there are also a handful of invoices for much larger amounts. In total, Trimmett and Co. has nearly £2,000 worth of overdue debt with you.

Arthur puts on his two-months-late voice. This, again, has been carefully crafted over decades and is calculated to instil mild anxiety in anyone who is of a less than iron disposition.

'Now look here, Mrs Platt', he says, 'this has gone on long enough. Why have you suddenly let all these invoices go overdue? We've got high standards in this company, you know. We're not prepared to deal with people who don't pay their bills when they're supposed to. What are you going to do about it?'

This time, Mrs Platt has her answer ready, though she stammers a bit because Arthur's intimidating techniques have had just the effect he knew they would.

'It's my manager, I'm afraid, Mr Beansprout,' she says apologetically. 'He says your sales department still haven't called round to replace the eyebolts and he's a bit fed up, so he told me not to pay any more of your invoices until the problem has been put right.'

'Hmm, we'll see about that,' says Arthur. He writes another memo to the sales department, but this time he writes it on pink paper so they'll be more likely to see it.

Another four weeks pass, and now the list of overdue Trimmett and Co. invoices is alarmingly long. It is three months since the first invoice, the one which caused all the trouble, was issued. Mrs Platt's manager has been steadfastly refusing to pay another penny until he gets his eyebolts. He is very annoyed and is threatening to take his business elsewhere. You ring up your sales department and order them to put their mistake right straightaway. You also speak to Arthur and ask him not to make any more credit control calls to Trimmett and Co. for the time being.

Arthur's colleagues are disappointed. It's not often that he gets to use his four-month voice. This is the one which includes the threat of criminal proceedings in the Old Bailey, and they always crowd round his telephone to listen when one of his virtuoso performances is taking place. It never fails to get results. Arthur is a very good credit controller.

Arthur Beansprout is, in case you had not already realized it, an illustration of the *negative attitude towards credit control.* He won't like it if you tell him to change what he considers effective methods which have clearly stood the test of time so well, but there are a number of things that need changing:

1 He only begins his credit control process *after the invoices become overdue.* It is bad enough for your cash flow that you have to give customers a month to pay in the first place, without the period of credit extending to two months or more in a case like this one. Arthur needs to be working on those invoices almost as soon as they have been issued and sent to the customer, and in any case well before they become due for payment.

2 He uses a tone of voice which varies from self-righteous to downright threatening. Although Mrs Platt falls for it, most customers would be annoyed by his aggressiveness and even less inclined to pay than they might be already. A little good old-fashioned *friendliness* would be a hundred times more effective.

3 He makes assumptions – in this case that, if Trimmett and Co. are not paying their invoices, it must be Trimmett and Co. that are in the wrong. He can see there is a problem, but it is part of his function to find out what that problem is and help sort it out in conjunction with the sales department. He should be *providing a service to the customer* – helping the customer to pay within your stated trading terms. He should be an integral part of the organization, not working in isolation.

At this point we are part of the way towards defining what your credit controllers can do for your company and how beneficial an effect they can have on your cash flow if they are properly trained and monitored. Of course, Arthur's example is something of an extreme one: he is dealing with a company which has a well-founded reason for wanting to withhold payment. More often, people are paying you late because there is some kind of inefficiency built into their system of paying, or simply because every day's delay in paying helps improve their own cash flow. Which of us, for example, can say we have never deliberately waited for the red reminder to arrive before paying a gas or electricity bill?

The essential thing in managing your own cash is that *you should be in control. You* should be carefully vetting anyone before you grant them credit. *You* should be keeping an eye on all your debtors and spotting those who may have trouble paying as soon as that month is up. *You* should be denying your customers any excuse for late payment, or non-payment, caused by weaknesses in the way you run your own company.

Of course, in a perfect world you would never have any overdue debt at all, and all your customers would be making sure their cheques were on your doormat at 9 a.m. on the day they were due. But there will always be factors which even the best of credit controllers cannot foresee or deal with. Nevertheless, if you find that some of the suggestions made in the following chapters would be suited to your company and its methods, you are virtually certain to be able to make substantial improvements in your cash flow, and ultimately in your profitability.

The purpose of this book is to show that it is easier and more beneficial, both to your company and your customers, to prevent debts becoming overdue in the first place, than to spend time and money chasing debts which have been allowed to become overdue. It is this use of the medicine to prevent, rather than cure the symptoms, which we call *the positive approach to cash collection.*

2 Putting your own house in order

As we have seen, the only way to improve your cash flow is to make your collection system more effective. The only way you are going to get your customers to pay you when you want them to is by *getting them on your side*. If you have their loyalty, you are going to be higher on their list of priorities when it comes to paying their debts. Conversely, it is no good reducing your sales ledger debt by driving away good customers who are frustrated by your inability to deal with their orders in an efficient manner.

Start with a complete review of all those areas of administration which affect your collection performance and have any kind of impact on the service you provide to your customers. This review needs to be carried out in an objective way so that any bad practices and habits which may have crept in over the years can be highlighted and then put right.

Many managers are under the firm impression that there is no room for improvement in their collection methods. In a few cases they are right: for example, firms which operate weekly or fortnightly collection and delivery cycles, or perhaps retail outlets or cash and carry operations. But if yours is one of the 90 per cent of companies which operate normal terms of trade, the chances are that at least some of your debts are not being paid when they should be, and that you could make a more efficient job of collecting cash than you do now. The methods described in this book are tried and tested ones which have brought lasting benefits to companies which have adopted them. Start from the principle that no customer is going to change a pattern of payment which it has developed, possibly over a number of years, unless you put your own house in order first. The first rule, therefore, is *not to give the customer any excuse for delaying payment or refusing to pay.*

Standing back and taking a critical look at your administrative systems and methods is not an easy process. It is part of human nature to find it difficult to admit our own faults, and we dislike other people telling us what we are doing wrong. Asking an employee to make a public admission that procedures they have evolved over long years with the company are unsound or inefficient is unlikely to get a positive response unless your approach is delicate and tactful. So, although the review process may be a painful one, it needs to be carried out honestly and objectively.

1 *View the company as an integral unit, not as a series of separate departments.* Like the engine of a car,

some parts may be functioning well, and others may need repair or replacement, but no component of the system functions totally independently of any other one. Don't let individual departments carry out their own reviews: it is a simple fact that very few of them will be able to be objective enough to see themselves as part of a larger organization.

2 *Be open about the fact that you are carrying out the review.* If there is one thing worse than having management looking over your shoulder and telling you where there is room for improvement, it is knowing that these shortcomings are being discussed behind your back. Your review cannot be a success unless it involves the whole of your management and staff. Discuss it openly with your department heads before it begins. This can be politically sensitive in some companies, but it is essential that you have everyone's cooperation. The improved cash flow resulting from the exercise will benefit every department, so you should explain these benefits and make sure that everyone knows what is expected of him or her. Any departmental barriers need to be gently but firmly broken down so that you can set up the best possible communication between departments.

3 *Consider the possibility of using an outside consultant* to carry out the review. This may well give you a better result and can be better for staff morale as well. Outside consultants have no axe to grind within the company. They are not hampered by departmental or political barriers and, unlike someone from inside the company, their normal duties will not suffer while they carry out the review. Also, the task can usually be carried out more speedily with less disruption to staff and their routines.

So it is vital to look at every part of the organization which has any connection with the sales, accounting and credit control process.

The sales and marketing departments

Sales and marketing are the departments which most often object to the review itself, and to the resulting changes in the way the company collects its debts. And yet, months later, when the review is over and has been acted upon, it is also these departments which gain most from it and which speak loudest in its support.

The fact is that the *improved relationships with customers* make your sales staff's job easier. They no longer have to waste time dealing with queries about late deliveries or missing documents every time they arrive on a customer's doorstep. Instead, they can get on with the job you employed them for: selling your products.

However, your sales staff have a very important role to play in the credit control process. It is they who meet your customer in the customer's shop, office or on the factory floor. This is the perfect opportunity for them, and you, to acquire a feel for the way your customer operates and the kind of person he is – in other words, whether or not he or she is someone you can feel happy about granting credit to. Of course, it is for the credit manager to decide who is to be granted credit, but any ruling should be made only after full consultation with the sales department.

The accounts and finance departments

These departments will be most affected by your changes, and in particular the sales ledger and credit control sections if they are separate in your organization. The staff will have to learn new collection techniques which may seem unorthodox, especially if they have been working for you for a long time.

It is often the case that the accounts and finance departments are to some extent isolated from the rest of the organization. If you are in the manufacturing business, they may even be invoicing customers for machinery or parts which they would not recognize if they tripped over them in the street. After all, what happens on the factory floor is not of any great concern to them.

One of your first tasks is to change this situation and make your accounts department an integral part of the organization, so that they are aware of progress and problems with your customers' orders and can answer directly to the customer about them. Your job is to *turn them into sales staff,* so that they, as well as the employees who go to see customers on their own premises, play a part in persuading customers that yours is a company they wish to continue dealing with and bring repeat business. Instead of simply reacting to situations as they arise (waiting for cheques to arrive and processing them, for example), they should be out there making sure those cheques are going to arrive when they are supposed to. Their role needs to be changed from a *passive* into an *active* one.

The depth of your review, and how long it takes to carry out, will vary from company to company. Appendix A at the end of this book (p. 95) lists the questions that need to be asked, and to whom they should be directed. It also describes how the findings of the review should be collated and communicated. The report that results from your review will form a *basis for discussion* by the people concerned. They and you should have an equal say in what happens next and how its results are to be translated into changes within your company. The report is only the first step towards more positive and effective management of your cash flow.

3 Credit control: where do you start?

Let us assume you have completed your review of the way your company works, as described in Chapter 2 and Appendix A. You have discussed its conclusions with the people concerned, heard their reactions and suggestions, and produced a final report. This has been acted on, and your company is now a sparkling new, well-oiled machine, all ready to go and get its sales ledger debt down as close to zero as makes no difference.

This chapter assumes that your company has a credit control section. Whether it consists of Mrs Suggs who comes in once a week to make a couple of dozen telephone calls, or a bank of twenty people with computer terminals and headsets, the principles are the same. The methods described in this and subsequent chapters can be adapted to any size of company. Even if there is no separate credit control function, and responsibility lies with the accounts department, the same principles hold true.

In Appendix A, we refer to the importance of analysing your sales ledger, with particular reference to an aged list of debtors. The latter has two functions:

(a) It shows you *how much debt there is available* to be turned into cash; and

(b) It tells you the *ratio of active accounts to the total sales ledger balance*. By active accounts, we mean those accounts on which transactions are taking place with some kind of regularity; you may want to include, say, any account on which there has been an entry during the last three months. You should also exclude accounts with small balances (less then £10, say), as these could distort your figures. The average ratio in Britain is about 80:20, meaning that 80 per cent of the sales ledger balance is owed by 20 per cent of the active acounts in the sales ledger for any given accounting period.

The latter figure should help you target those customers you are going to contact during the month. Normally, it is not going to be practicable to telephone every single active customer in the sales ledger; you simply will not have the time or the staff available. Instead, if you can work out which customers fall into that 20 per cent of accounts, and your collection techniques are effective, you should be able to create a substantial improvement to the 80 per cent of the total balance they represent.

Of course, this is not to say that you will be ignoring the remaining accounts just because they have small balances. What you *will* be doing is contacting them less frequently and not spending any more time on them than is justified by their magnitude.

Of the 20 per cent (or whatever the percentage is in your particular case), *every account* (not just those which are overdue) will be contacted at least once a month. This will mean different amounts of work for different companies. You may only be dealing with three or four companies, each of which owes you a large amount of money; in this case, there is less that you can do towards improving your cash flow. But the advantage of this technique is its flexibility to suit different types of company.

These contacts should preferably be *by telephone.* Unless you are able to appear smiling, and cap in hand, on all your customers' doorsteps once a month, there is no more effective way of collecting cash. You can send begging letters until you are blue in the face, but if the person at the other end is determined to use your letters as a lining for his or her 'Pending' tray you are wasting time and money. Provided you can get through on the telephone to the person you want to speak to, there is no way they can escape your clutches – they *have* to give you some kind of response, even if it is a negative one. But if your credit control system is working properly, you will be able to gain their genuine commitment to come up with some money, and they will honour that commitment.

The flexibility of this method lies also in the fact that, each month, the credit control manager can assess:

(a) How much debt there is to collect; and
(b) How many staff, and how much time, he or she has available to collect that debt.

So, for example, if half the staff had fallen victim to a 'flu epidemic and the amount to be collected was unusually high in any given month, the staff could be told to contact accounts only if they had a balance of more than £1,000. When the situation improved in the following month, this minimum could be reduced to £500.

The management will therefore need to spend an hour or two at the beginning of each month looking at an aged sales ledger. They will identify the *X* per cent of accounts they want to tackle, and then they are in a position to set themselves and their staff a *monthly work plan* and *collection targets.*

There are almost always varying degrees of resistance to this idea. To some employees, it will smack too much of Five-Year Plans and daily quotas. They will need a great deal of reassurance, and they need to understand that this is not a means of checking that they are all pulling their weight, but that it simply provides a yardstick to measure themselves against. It is no use saying that your collection performance is either good or bad unless you know what you were expecting it to be and have something to compare the actual figure to. Likewise, you need to be able to establish trends from month to month so that you can gauge the effectiveness of your collection methods. It will probably take time, but eventually your staff will understand what it is all for and react enthusiastically to it.

So the work plan should chart an acceptable workload for each member of staff, beginning on the day that information about the sales ledger becomes available. Do not simply throw it on to the relevant desk and expect the staff member to get on with it. Discuss it with him or her and if he or she feels strongly that any of the figures are unrealistic, change them.

MONTHLY WORK PLAN

Week Commencing	Monday	Tuesday	Wednesday	Thursday	Friday
August 2	------STATEMENTS------ Correspondence Cash allocation	Correspondence Cash allocation	Correspondence Cash allocation 5 calls high value accounts	Cash allocation 15 calls high value accounts Correspondence	10 calls high value accounts Cash allocation Reconciliations
August 9	Cash allocation 10 calls high value accounts	Cash allocation 20/25 calls high value accounts	Cash allocation 20/25 calls high value accounts	Cash allocation 20/25 calls high value accounts	Cash allocation 10 calls high value accounts Reconciliations
August 16	Cash allocation Correspondence 20 calls high value accounts		2nd letter Cash allocation Follow up calls	2nd letter Cash allocation Follow up calls	2nd letter Cash allocation Follow up calls
August 23				Cash allocation Correspondence Reconciliation	Cash allocation Reconciliation
August 30	Bank holiday				

Figure 3.1 *A typical monthly work plan*

An example of a typical work plan is shown in Figure 3.1. You can easily adapt this, and all the other forms in this book, at very little cost.

At the end of each day, each member of the collection staff will need to fill in details of his or her actual performance. The exact format of this report, and how the whole system works, is described in more detail in Chapter 9.

Armed with your list of the major accounts in descending order of value, you can now get your staff to telephone customers in that order. In other words, the criterion you are now using to decide on the importance of an account is *its value, not its age.* This is not to say that you will not be trying your hardest to collect the smaller balances as well, and in Chapter 8 we have given suggestions as to how to deal with these.

Initially this will probably go against the grain with your collectors. Why should they be chasing Arbuckle and Co. for a £600 invoice that's not even due for payment yet, when Mr Firkin of Firkin and Partners has been deliberately dragging his heels about paying a £90 invoice due three months ago, in the hope that you'll write it off rather than take him to court?

It will take perhaps three months for this system to gain acceptance and start working properly. The timescale is normally something along these lines:

Month 1 Carry out the review of the way the company works, and act on it.

Month 2 Retrain credit controllers in your new approach to collecting debt and get them accustomed to it. At this stage there will probably be some improvement in your collection performance, but nothing to write home about.

Month 3 Put your philosophy across to your customers and gain their acceptance of it. Only now will you start to see really tangible benefits in the amount of cash you collect.

In the following months, as the enthusiasm of your staff and customers for the new system grows, you will start to wonder how you ever managed under the *ancien régime*. But don't assume that everything will neatly slot into place: you should constantly be sounding people out as to whether the new system is working and what they think of it. It will take perhaps nine months of close liaison and supervision before it has become ingrained in everyone who is involved. But, at last, you have begun a change in emphasis. It is *you* who now control the amount of cash received each month, not your customers.

4 Knowing your customers

If you have been trading for any length of time, an awareness of your customers and their needs should already be built into the system. The chances are that it is your sales or marketing departments that know your customers best. They will be aware of your customers' buying habits, so that they are not wasting time calling on them when there is no point in your manufacturing round holes if your customer has square pegs to fit them into.

What companies often neglect, though, is customer awareness on the part of their credit controllers as well. If Trimmett and Co. faithfully produce all their cheques on the 23rd of each month, there is no point in Arthur Beansprout contacting them on the 22nd and asking for payment of your invoices. Or, to use another example, if you have just sent them a £10,000 consignment of goods and you know that it takes them a week to process your invoices, Arthur should not be just getting round to sending out the invoice for £10,000 on the 20th, when it will miss their deadline and not be paid until a month later.

So, when Arthur picks up the telephone to the customer, he should know *who does what, when and why*. He will need to know facts like these:

- Who processes, and who approves your invoices?
- Who prepares, signs and posts the cheques used to pay you?
- Is there an order number or reference number which will speed up payment of the invoice if you quote it?
- What is the latest date in the month when you can safely send your customer an invoice and know that it will be input, checked and approved in time for their next cheque run?

See Chapter 6 to find out how and where to obtain this information.

If he has all this information at his fingertips, Arthur will know at any particular stage during the month whom he should be contacting and where he can get hold of them. This will save him time and money which would otherwise be spent in frustrating searches for the right person in a company with, say, 800 or 1,000 staff, and which leaves him short-tempered and less effective when he finally does find them. Simple little details like this are an essential part of a positive approach to collecting cash.

Not only does this knowledge make Arthur more efficient, it also gets the customer on his side from the outset. If he simply asks to speak to the bought ledger department each time he gets through to a customer, and the customer does not even have a department of that name, the telephone call is going to be twice as long as it needs to be.

All this vital information needs to be on paper somewhere within Arthur's reach. If you deal with a large number of customers, you may want to put their details on to a database package on a PC. Alternatively, a simple card index would probably do the job just as well. Figure 4.1 shows a suggested layout for the form, with one per customer.

If there are large numbers of customers, you could start by recording *customer details* of those who fall within the 20 per cent category explained in Chapter 3, and eventually extend this to all your customers. Exactly how much detail it goes into will depend on the size of your company and the size of the average company you are dealing with, but it will probably include the following:

- Customer's name and address
- The address invoices and statements should go to, if this is different
- The number of their account in your sales ledger
- Their credit limit, and the date it was agreed or changed
- The full name, job title, department and extension number of everyone who has a hand in the process of paying your invoices
- Their cut-off date for processing invoices
- Any other important information, such as extended credit facilities, or any other variation in your normal terms of trade.

CUSTOMER CONTACT AND HISTORY FORM			
Account number		Credit limit	
Name		Telephone numbers	
Address 1		Address 2	
Contact 1		Position	
Contact 2		Position	
Finance director			
Payment schedule			
Account instructions			

Date	Notes	Action

Figure 4.1 *Customer contact and history form*

On a separate section of the form, you should record a *customer history*. This will show very brief details of each contact made by Arthur with the customer, as follows:

(a) whether it was by phone, letter, telex or other method of communication;
(b) the contents of the contact, including any promises made by the customer (e.g. 'Cheque signer on holiday. Full payment by 23/6');
(c) an action or diary section for any further follow-up that may be needed.

There are two reasons why you need this record of contacts with your customer. The first is that it establishes stability. This will be useful long after Arthur has been poached by a head-hunting company or hit by a runaway Centurion tank. Even if he is simply ill for a week, someone else can confidently step into his shoes and do the job just as effectively as he does, without having to start all over again and possibly aggravate customers by asking for information which Arthur has already obtained.

Second, it creates a diary of events which can be used in conjunction with the monthly work plan. Suppose Trimmett and Co. tell Arthur that there has been a slight delay in payment because you still have not got round to issuing a credit note which they're planning to offset against the amount they owe you. Arthur can now make a note to himself to check in two weeks' time (a) that the credit note has gone out to Trimmett and Co. and (b) that they have paid up. Even if the credit note has not been sent to them, he should ring back in two weeks' time and at least apologize for the delay. Not only is this basic courtesy, it also builds up the feeling in your customer that you trust them and they can rely on you as well. If Arthur has established a sufficiently good rapport with them, they will even pay you anyway and deduct the value of the credit note, knowing they can expect to receive it when Arthur said they would.

The one thing to remember is that, if it is your company that is at fault and it is your oversight that is causing a delay in your customer's payment, you should acknowledge the fact rather than try to cover it up. Your customers will respect you for your frankness.

If it is Trimmett and Co. that are causing the hold-up, and they agree to put the matter right by a certain date, Arthur can now telephone them on that date if the payment is still not forthcoming. He can give them a gentle but firm reminder of their previous conversation, and knows exactly how much they promised to pay and when.

The use of a form to record important information about your customer, and details of Arthur's dealings with them, is a hundredfold improvement over the system still in use by far too many companies – that of jotting down notes on the nearest scrap of paper that comes to hand and promptly losing it.

Many companies prefer to have all this information in the sales ledger itself. This is an equally effective method, although it can mean that, if your sales ledger fills up at all quickly, you have to transfer information from the old to the current pages of the ledger. Not only does this waste time, it involves the risk of overlooking an important message.

When you have been operating this system for a while, you will have a clear picture of each customer and their payment habits. If they promise to pay you by a certain date, you will have a reasonable idea whether or not that promise can be relied upon. If they cannot be relied on, and you are constantly having to remind them of their omissions, they cannot argue with a detailed written record of these omissions. Sooner or later, they will learn to stop giving you misleading information or excuses and start paying you in accordance with your stated terms and conditions. The system will also allow you to set a realistic credit limit whenever you wish to review how much credit you grant to each customer.

Each time a new customer comes into the fold, make sure that one of these forms is completed from the very outset. Ideally, the information should be provided by the sales representative who introduced the new customer. Failing this, it is an ideal excuse for Arthur to get to know his opposite number in the customer's bought ledger department. Either way, the form needs to be completed before you start credit to the customer. Whichever method you use, the fact of being asked these questions will help to convince the customer of your professionalism. You are going to give them what they want, when they want it.

You might even want to embody this information in the application form for credit, described in Chapter 10. Apart from saving paper, it means you have absolutely everything you need to know about the customer together in one place.

Arthur is now well armed with information about the company at the other end of the telephone line, confident and *almost* ready to make his first new-style telephone call.

5 Getting ready for the telephone call

There are probably two main points of contact between you and your customers. The first is likely to be your sales department. Their approach will be a positive one: they have to persuade your customers that your firm, and not your competitors, is who they want to deal with. Part of this positive approach is that they go into it prepared: they know the background to your previous dealings, if any, with the customer, and they have an idea what the customer is likely to be looking for in the future.

The other point of contact is likely to be your accounts department, and in particular your credit controllers. All too often this tends to be of a negative, even threatening nature, with little thought of the effect it will have on longer-term relations between you and the customer.

Work on the assumption that *every call to the customer is a sales call.* Every contact, no matter how trivial, goes to form part of the image the customer has of you. Every call will affect the likelihood of their bringing you repeat business in the future. People have short memories: very often, you are only as good as your last telephone call.

Likewise, although the telephone is by far the most effective means of collecting cash (short of knocking on the customer's door), it is only as good as the person using it. It can also be one of the most misused and neglected items of equipment in the collector's armoury; all too often, people will much rather write another pompous letter to a debtor than pick up the receiver and talk to them direct.

Arthur Beansprout used to be a Good Credit Controller, but now he is an Even Better Credit Controller. Ever since you sat down with him for a chat, told him how pleased you were with his performance and suggested various methods he might use to become even more effective, he's been reacting very positively. One thing that particularly made a difference was the fact that you have promised to pay him a performance-related bonus on top of his normal salary. But he also likes the fact that you're paying attention to him and his job, and the new methods you've taught him have added a great deal of spice to what was starting to become a somewhat tedious way of paying his mortgage and feeding the wife and kids.

He now has the monthly work plan you agreed with him taped up on the wall in front of him. It's Monday morning, and the work plan says '15 calls to high value accounts'. The Manchester branch of the Kuwaiti Snowshoe Company, or KSC as it is normally known, owes you just under £15,000 (though most of it is not due for payment until ten days' time), and they are the first company he is going to call.

Apart from the half-empty packet of Benson and Hedges and the obligatory photo of his wife, he has two pieces of paper and a pen on his desk.

The first, and most important piece of paper is a copy of the current month's statement for KSC. He has glanced at it, and has seen that the balance is made up of six invoices, copies of which are attached to the back of the statement. He has a look at these, and makes sure that the totals tally with the statement.

The second is the customer history form for KSC. There is nothing written in the space for details of contacts with the customer, because they have been good payers most of the time and he has not called them before. He is not sure exactly which member of staff he should be talking to. But they are known to be a reliable company, and they are well within their credit limit of £20,000. There have not been any problems or queries raised by the customer which might lead to a delay in their paying you.

He pauses for a minute and gazes out of the window, running through in his mind what he wants to say to the company. Then he takes a piece of scrap paper from the drawer and writes down the main points he wants to raise with them, just in case he misses anything out while on the phone. These he can tick off the list as he deals with them.

Finally (and he's still slightly embarrassed about doing this, but it was what you agreed), he *smiles.* Although it sounds silly, and the person at the other end cannot see him doing it, the frame of mind it reflects comes across loud and clear down the telephone line. A cheerful, friendly attitude will receive a cheerful, friendly response. If the call sounds sullen or depressed, or it sounds like the ninety-seventh call he has made that day, then at best they are going to pay less attention to what he has to say than they otherwise would.

Although the routine is a new one as far as Arthur is concerned, it is becoming more ingrained in him with every passing day. He can see that being properly prepared before he dials KSC's number, and not wasting time hunting for information, is reaping considerable and tangible benefits already.

6 Collecting by telephone

You now have most of your new collection system in place, and your customers are about to see it in action as Arthur starts telephoning them. But they should not have to learn about it implicitly, simply by noticing the change in your style of dealing with them and forming their own conclusions from it. You have to *educate* the customer, and you may have to persuade them to make changes in the way they normally deal with you.

This chapter is divided into two sections. The first suggests how you should introduce your customers to your new methods and collect the information you need to fill in the blanks on your customer details form if necessary. The second shows how to make follow-up calls and ensure that the system becomes an integral and effective part of your company's strategy.

Both parts could be converted into a 'script' for your employees to work from. This is not to say that they should be sitting there all day delivering stereotyped monologues into the unwilling ears of your customers, but a large proportion of their calls will tend to follow a similar pattern and they may find it useful and time-saving to have a ready-made checklist telling them the main items they need to cover. Obviously, if they use a script, they are free to adapt it to suit their own style and to the degree of subtlety required in speaking to the customer.

The first call

The first time Arthur contacts KSC, he will not be asking for money at all. His purpose is twofold. He needs to tell the customer about your new approach to collecting cash, and he needs to gather the rest of the information he needs for the customer details form. When he has done this, he might decide it is a suitable opportunity to talk about payments as well, but the chances are he will have taken up so much of the customer's time on the phone already that this would be the right moment to end the call.

The procedure he follows is something along these lines.

He introduces himself, giving his full name (with the emphasis on the first name) and what he does.

He establishes whom he is talking to and that they are the people he should be dealing with in the future. Unless they prefer to be known as Mr or Mrs or Ms So-and-So, he tries to get on to first-name terms as soon as possible without being artificially friendly. This means that, ideally, they become friends as well as business contacts. This makes them more responsive to you and your message; it also helps Arthur gain more enjoyment from his job. Perhaps most importantly, it makes use of the fact that people find it hard to say 'no' to friends, whether being asked for money or any other favour.

He explains why he is calling. He tells them that your company has embarked on a new system of customer service, and that he (Arthur) has been given greater independence as well as personal responsibility for handling their account. But he still has to make a monthly report to you, his manager, and would welcome any help they may be able to give him. As part of this new philosophy of giving a better service to the customer, he is expected to become familiar with his customers' staff and the way they operate.

Of course, if KSC is fed up to the back teeth with what seems to be your company's inability to provide the right products at the right time, their response to statements like these is likely to be a cynical one. But Arthur can use this to his advantage by agreeing with them, even if it puts your company in a bad light. This will help to relax the person he is talking to and make them more responsive to what he has to say.

He builds up a picture of the customer's business. This will include:

1 what they do with your invoices and statements;
2 which members of staff, in which departments, deal with each part of the payment process;
3 whether there are certain days in the month put aside to process invoices, or whether they are dealt with as they are received

He needs to obtain an overall view of what would happen to an invoice which arrived on KSC's doormat tomorrow. Whose hands would it pass through? How long does it take to produce a cheque?

Finally, Arthur explains that *you now have a new system for resolving queries* about goods or invoices you have sent them. This will mean that problems will be identified as soon as they arise and dealt with as quickly as possible, rather than being left to drift as they were before. This process may even involve Arthur's telephoning before an invoice is due for payment, to make sure there are no queries which might delay its being paid.

This is a great deal of information to elicit and communicate in one telephone call, which is why it is recommended that Arthur leave any discussions about payment until later on. Of course, if KSC do bring up a query or problem during the conversation, or if they mention payment without being prompted, then he can follow the matter through to its conclusion.

As Arthur is contacting only 20 per cent or so of your active customers, there should be plenty of time to contact them later on in the month about the money they owe you. As we mentioned previously, you are unlikely to experience any improvement in the amount of cash you collect during the first month or two of operating the new system; it will almost certainly deteriorate for a while.

The second and subsequent calls

Once Arthur has filled in all the empty spaces on his customer information forms, he is a more effective collector because he knows when in the month to call a specific customer and whom he should speak to. Next time he speaks to KSC, he will be talking about the entire balance on their account, whether or not it is overdue.

This next call will probably be in the middle of the first month of operating the new system. In subsequent months, the customers should be contacted on a regular basis, ideally during the early part of the month so that there is plenty of time for any problems to be resolved before it is time for them to pay you. Once the contact becomes part of the monthly routine, and Arthur has established friendly relations with the people he deals with, they will be ready and waiting to give him details of how much they plan to pay and when.

The best time of all to phone them is a day or two after you have sent out your statements. These, in turn, should be going out immediately after your financial month-end; if they are not, you should also put this right.

The first thing Arthur asks is whether they have received (a) the statement itself and (b) all the invoices it refers to. If they have, the next question is whether they have any queries or problems relating to the invoices themselves or the goods they represent. If they say 'yes', he then takes down the full details and promises that the query will be resolved by a certain date. These details go onto a query form which he passes on to the relevant department to deal with.

If the customer says that one or more of the invoices are missing, he checks the date that they were sent. It is possible they were sent out recently and have not had enough time to be processed and arrive on your contact's desk. If they do not fall into this category, he obtains copies and sends them off first class. A letter to accompany them takes time and does not really achieve anything, so a simple handwritten note on a compliments slip is fine. He also checks whether photocopies will do; many customers will ask for the invoice to be re-issued, as they cannot claim VAT from a copy invoice.

Finally, Arthur records brief details of the conversation on the 'customer history' section of the customer information sheet. Time will tell whether the customer has been using delaying tactics or not.

If all is well and the customer has processed all the invoices you have sent them, the balance on the statement will agree with the balance on their bought ledger. This amount should be what they intend to pay you when they carry out their next cheque run. Note that, so far, Arthur has not made any request for money: he has simply ensured that what they think they owe you and what you think they owe you are one and the same figure.

Provided the balances are the same, he can ask when they plan to post you a cheque for the amount agreed. If this date is close to your month-end, he may need politely to insist that they post it first class. Alternatively, the customer may be willing to deliver it in person or, if it is large enough to make it worth your while, you might wish to collect it – perhaps by courier.

Having now established that KSC intends to pay the agreed amount at the agreed time, Arthur also has to make sure that there are no invoices which are still in the customer's system and are waiting to be approved for payment. This may well involve speaking to another link in the chain. Here there is another opportunity for the customer to raise any queries they may have over your invoices. If they do, Arthur records it on his customer information form and sends a query form off to the department concerned.

Of course, the customer may flatly say that it is not convenient for them to adhere to your payment terms because they operate a different system to yours. If there is any room for compromise (such as sending out statements earlier), then Arthur will use it. If the worst comes to the worst, though, he will have to insist politely but firmly that it is a condition of your granting credit that they pay when you ask them to.

Never forget that people who work in bought ledger departments are by and large typical of the human race in that they will do anything for a quiet life. They prefer their work to be as easy and trouble-free as possible. Their job is to make sure your account is approved and paid as quickly as possible, with the minimum of trouble. The majority of them have no interest in cash flow problems, and they have nothing to gain by delaying payment of your account. The accounts that give them the least trouble will be dealt with first; those suppliers who create problems for them will tend to get shoved to the bottom of a foot-high pile of paper and forgotten about. If Arthur can help to make their jobs easier, they will welcome it.

By this point, there is little reason why Arthur should not receive KSC's cheque when they say he will, but he still makes a diary note to himself to check. He has now started building up a history of their payment habits for future reference and, as the months go by, he will have a fairly clear idea whether they are the type of company who proffer genuine reasons, rather than excuses, when they are late in paying.

Arthur will also be in a better position to spot real problems when they do arise and tackle them in their infancy, before they grow to unmanageable proportions. It may be, for example, that someone is not paying you because they simply do not have the money to do so. If this is a short-term situation, a post-dated cheque, or series of cheques, may be the solution. If the problem is more serious and long-term, you will need more precise details. Because there is a relationship of trust, they should be fairly forthcoming provided you emphasize that you are trying to help them, as well as yourself.

This is a time when liaison between the accounts and sales departments is particularly needed so that a close eye can be kept on the customer. If their problems are resolvable, you might want to allow them to pay back what they owe in instalments over a longer period of time, if possible using post-dated cheques. At the same time, the sales department needs to keep a watch on their future orders, so that they can continue trading but not increase the amount of money they owe you.

Assuming this setback is overcome eventually, you will probably have gained a great deal of respect and loyalty from them. If you rush off to the nearest court the moment the alarm bells start to sound, you may be missing an opportunity to help your customer through a crisis and strengthen the relationship between you. If the customer is a large one who is giving you a great deal of business, you could be harming yourself if you are too precipitate.

Of course, there will come a time when it will be clear that a customer is headed for disaster, and then you will need to act promptly to make sure they are not sold any more goods which will increase their indebtedness to you. In this situation, avoid recriminations and bitterness which can only be self-destructive. You may well need to apply considerable pressure, even to the extent of involving outside debt collectors or taking the customer to court, but this should always be a last resort.

Customers are your life-blood. They can be very hard to gain, but all too easy to upset and lose. Give them the service they deserve and they will respond not only by paying your account, but by giving you more business. If you make your approach a friendly and positive one, even in time of trouble, they will be receiving a service that your competitors probably do not provide.

7 Problem customers

Human nature being what it is, there will be a handful of customers to whom your new way of collecting money will not make an iota of difference. They will happily carry on as they always have, giving bill-payment a somewhat lower priority than watering the office cactus.

At this point, restraint on your part becomes marginally less important. If a customer is deliberately delaying payment, and there are other people besides yourself hammering on their door, it is the person who hammers loudest who is most likely to get paid. So you need to start the process as early as possible in the month, and keep up constant pressure. If this means telephoning every two days for two weeks, then so be it. Likewise, if you are unable to get through to the specific person dealing with the payment of your account, then talk to anyone. The more they hear your name and your voice, the better. If you have to leave a message because you cannot talk to the right person, then realize that the onus is on you to try again if they do not call back. Remember, too, that if attention is being focused on them it means they may not be able to get away with it as far as other suppliers are concerned either, so it is in their interest to stay out of the limelight.

Shouting or hostility will not work; these will land you in an even less favourable situation than before you started. The solution, quite simply, is persistence and gentle, but firm, prodding. Never accept any excuse right away, but talk the problem over with the customer. It's surprising how quickly some excuses evaporate.

You are engaged in a battle of wits by this stage, and certain weapons are permissible which would be regarded as unstatesmanlike in a less difficult situation. There is no reason why you should not start to use ploys similar to those the customer is using. The following are a few examples: with a little imagination, you should be able to come up with a few more yourself.

'As a favour to me': Once you have established a personal relationship with the person on the other end of the phone, you can play on this friendship. For example, a cheque may have been held up in the customer's bought ledger department. If you can get your credit controller to ask for the cheque to be hurried up as a personal favour (perhaps because you are ostensibly breathing down their neck), this minor mendacity can work wonders.

'End of month': Tell the offender that a certain date is the end of your accounting period and that only

money which comes though the door by that date will be counted as having been collected during this month. Could they make a special effort this week and help you out?

'End of year': An extension of the above approach, but to be used only when it is more or less true. This particular pretext should be used with care; it can be somewhat transparent on closer examination, and if the customer sees through it, it can lose what little goodwill may remain between you. You could also say that you are coming up to the end of the fiscal quarter.

This pretext can work particularly well with local authorities and government departments, who are a little less worldly-wise about the machinations of commerce than others. Of course, it is very important that the credit controller makes a note of the pretext on the customer history form, so that it is not over-used.

'Cash forecasting': This is a serious-sounding approach, which further enhances the impression that you are operating advanced credit control techniques (which, of course, you are). You have 'forecast' that you will collect a certain amount by a certain date this month, and you want to be absolutely certain you will make it. How much is the customer planning to send, and when?

This leaves your customer with a sense of obligation; if they have not sent what they owe you, they have let you down. Most people have at least the rudiments of a conscience, and this particular story will tug at least a little at most people's heartstrings. Also, many customers will not be able to tell you off the cuff how much they owe you and will have to put themselves out a bit to answer your question. If the exercise is made to sound important enough, they will not wish to appear incompetent in the face of what is such an obviously professional company as yours.

'The Auditors': Every department of your customer's company that deals with money in some shape or form will be subject to the scrutiny of the dreaded auditors. The chances are, therefore, that the person you deal with will be aware of what an eternal nuisance they are.

You are sorry to trouble them, but their account has been picked at random by the auditors whilst checking that your credit control procedures are up to scratch. Please could they send you a cheque by a specified date; this will help to ensure that the auditors go away satisfied and leave you in peace for another six or twelve months.

'Monthly statements': It is possible that your computer has sent out some incorrect statements this month; it's not the first time it has happened. The mistake may be in the customer's favour. Please could the customer check their copy against the invoices they have and see whether they agree with it or not?

They will come back to you and say that they cannot see anything wrong with it. They have fallen hook line and sinker for your ploy; if they agree the amount, they are presumably about to send a cheque for that amount. Could they confirm that it is on its way and when you can expect to receive it, please?

In this battle of wits, you are more likely to come out on top than the customer. Persistence, firmness, politeness (and the occasional white lie) will always win out in the end.

8 What to do with the small account

Small customers are expensive to look after. It is expensive to send out salespeople to keep them happy and supplied with your products; it is expensive in terms of postage or transport costs to get the products to them; and it is expensive to try and recoup the money if their accounts are overdue.

In most businesses, it is not going to be possible to make contact with every single account by telephone each month, which is why in previous chapters we have focused on the collection of large accounts. If, after servicing these accounts, you still have time and resources left over, you could start on some of the higher-value smaller accounts.

But what about a customer who owes you £25? Small though this account may be, if there are enough of the same size they will represent a substantial asset to your company.

This is where the letter comes into its own. Of course, it can never be as effective, or flexible, as the personal approach, principally because of its predictability. Most companies have a regular cycle of letters to deal with overdue accounts. Almost always, they share the following features:

- They are sent to *all* customers, irrespective of the size of the account (everyone knows someone who has received a threatening letter asking for an overdue balance of 5p).
- They always say the same thing.
- They are usually sent 10 or 14 days apart.
- They do not start being sent until the invoice has become overdue.

Because this routine is so predictable, the customer quickly gets wise to the procedure the company follows with overdue accounts and realizes that it is quite safe to ignore the first one or two letters (remember the red reminder on your electricity bill?). They are thus taking advantage of a source of interest-free, unauthorized credit. The account can be 60 days or more overdue before the company starts to stir itself into taking any serious action.

If you use letters to collect debts, *change them.* Change the *content,* the *style* and the *date you send them* at least three or four times during the course of the year. Keep customers constantly on their toes by not allowing any pattern to emerge that they will be able to detect and profit from.

Also, *make the letter look individual.* You probably know from your own experience that if you receive a photocopy of a photocopy of a letter, with your name and address written in by hand, you are less likely to pay any attention to it than if it has an impressive coloured letterheading and looks as though it has been individually and personally typed to you. Far too little use is being made of word processors for reminder letters.

One TV rental company was sending out several thousand invoices each month, all for one year's rental. The amounts involved were small and, because they were annual invoices, it was impossible to establish any form of regular contact with their customers: each month, a different batch of people was being invoiced. For this company, postal collection was the only answer. One variation that they used was simply to change to red ink for their monthly statements. This simple alteration convinced their customers that the statement was a final demand, and a much higher than usual proportion of them paid up promptly. After the initial success of this idea, they experimented with inks of other colours as well. This example shows how effective variation of colour, form and content can be when collecting money by letter.

The first letter you send out should be both exploratory and informative, as were the first telephone calls to higher-value accounts. It should tell your customer the following.

1 Your terms of trade, in case they have forgotten.
2 The fact that you now have an improved system for collecting cash and dealing with their queries.
3 The full name, telephone number and extension of the credit controller responsible for their account.

The letter also has to find out the information you need to complete a customer information form for the customer. It is unlikely to be very detailed, as you will not be contacting the customer as frequently as a larger account, but you should ask at least for the name and extension number of a contact and details of when they pay their invoices. Do this on a tear-off form so that the customer is involved in the minimum of expense and trouble.

Emphasize, too, that if their queries are to be dealt with effectively they need to be with you as soon as possible after they receive the invoice. Give them a week, or at most ten days, so that you can sort out the problem in time to be paid during the current month and not miss the boat until four weeks later. State clearly that if an invoice has not been queried by the end of this period, then the customer must pay its full value. This is, of course, without prejudice to any of their rights should the invoice prove to have been wrong.

The reason for specifying this period is that it takes longer for you to become aware of a customer's query if it is by post. With the telephone you know about it, and can act on it, as soon as the customer is telephoned at the beginning of the month. Figure 8.1 shows a suggested format for this introductory letter.

Figures 8.2, 8.3 and 8.4 show a suggested first, second and third letter to be sent to each customer. Each bears a tear-off portion for the customer to give details of payments made (a remittance advice) and a space for queries.

The *first letter* is purely a request, not a demand. It introduces the credit controller and asks for the information you need.

The *second letter* is a reminder, asking for payment before a certain date and stating the consequences of non-payment by that date (whether future deliveries of goods will be suspended, or some other form of action taken). You should be strict about

CUSTOMERS NAME Date

Dear

ACCOUNT NO:

You have been a valued customer of this company for some time, and I am writing to tell you of changes we have made to improve the service we give to you.

I am now personally responsible for your account, and my name is .... If you have any cause at all to contact me, you are welcome to do so by telephoning me on .... ext .... As I now have more independence and responsibility for your account, I will now be able to respond to your queries much more quickly than in the past. We have also introduced a system for monitoring the progress of your queries and ensuring they are resolved as quickly as possible.

To help me maintain this improved service, I would appreciate it if, should you have any queries about invoices sent to you which might delay payment, you contact me within *seven days* of receiving the invoice. This is in fact one of the terms of our granting credit to you, and could mean that if your query is not raised with us within that period you will be liable for the full balance on your account.

Also as part of this improved service to our customers, I have been asked by our senior management to become as familiar as possible with your staff and your operating procedures. Your help in completing and returning the enclosed questionnaire in the reply-paid envelope would be greatly appreciated. This will help me to build an accurate picture of your business and put me in a better position to understand your problems and requirements in the future.

Thank you very much for your help.

Yours sincerely,

CREDIT CONTROLLER

Figure 8.1 *Suggested introductory letter*

CUSTOMER'S NAME Date

Dear

RE: ACCOUNT NO:
ACCOUNT BALANCE:

I have pleasure in enclosing a statement for the above account. I would ask that you carefully check this statement to the invoices in your possession. If you disagree with any item on the statement, please let me know on the slip below within seven days.

If I do not receive any query from you within that time, I shall assume that you will be paying the full balance on the statement. I would remind you that under the terms and conditions of our credit agreement, you are liable for the full amount if you do not express written disagreement within seven days of this letter.

Thank you very much for your cooperation.

Yours sincerely,

CREDIT CONTROLLER

....

ACCOUNT NO .... £..................
CHEQUE ENCLOSED FOR £..............
PAYMENT IS BEING WITHHELD BECAUSE..........................
....
SIGNED............................... DATE...............................
POSITION........................... TEL. NO..........................

Please list the invoices your payment represents on the back of this slip.

Figure 8.2 *Suggested first letter*

CUSTOMER'S NAME Date

Dear

RE: ACCOUNT NO:
ACCOUNT BALANCE

I am surprised to note that I do not appear to have had any response to my previous letter. As you have not raised any query about this account, I will be expecting to receive payment of the full balance on the account within five days of your receiving this letter. If you should have any queries relating to the balance they will be dealt with, but I require payment in full now. Any overpayment you make will be refunded in due course.

Yours sincerely,

CREDIT CONTROLLER

(Enclose payment/query advice slip as in first letter)

Figure 8.3 *Suggested second letter*

CUSTOMER'S NAME Date

Dear

RE: ACCOUNT NO.
ACCOUNT BALANCE

I am surprised to note that you still have not responded to my two previous letters, and although I have made every effort to assist you, you have not settled your account. If I have not received payment by return of post, this company will no longer supply any goods to you and the matter will be passed to our solicitors for legal action, without further reference to you.

Yours sincerely,

CREDIT CONTROLLER

(Enclose payment/query advice slip as in first letter)

Figure 8.4 *Suggested final letter*

carrying out what your letter says you will: it is better to make no threats at all than empty ones which you have no intention of pursuing. As soon as you start doing so, the customer will cease to take you seriously and you have lost your controlling position. This applies equally, of course, to telephone calls.

The *third and final letter* should always be preceded by a phone call. There should be few accounts each month that have reached this stage and need contacting. If this call also proves unsatisfactory, or simply does not produce a genuine reason for non-payment of the account, the third letter must be sent. It will clearly and firmly state the action you intend to take to recover the debt, whether this be using outside debt collectors or taking the customer to court; the latter will involve the customer in additional trouble and expense. By this stage, you no longer need to consider the customer's feelings: you can afford not to do any further business with this type of person or company.

Promptness is of the essence with all of these letters. They need to be produced as soon as possible after the end of the month, and you should send the larger accounts by first-class post. If your letter cycle is streamlined enough, you will save one or two days at the beginning of the month and prevent a number of accounts becoming overdue in your sales ledger.

As with the larger accounts, it is important to keep a history of your contacts with the smaller customer and to diarize future contacts. If necessary, begin with the largest small accounts and work downwards.

On the other hand, you may come to the conclusion that it simply is not worth your while to spend any money collecting these small balances.

One solution to this situation would be to divide them into geographical areas and appoint one of the largest and most reliable of your customers in that area as an agent or distributor. A small customer may be uneconomical for you, as a large or medium-sized company, to service. For a smaller business, the opposite may apply.

It may be that your agent or distributor initially requires financial or operational help, perhaps in the form of extended credit. However, the cost of providing this is often far outweighed by the saving in cost to you. Your collection department will have more time to devote to the larger accounts, and other areas of your company will also appreciate the savings to be made. One of the disadvantages is that you are increasing the amount of commercial risk you are involved in, and the process of selecting and monitoring your agent needs to be a very careful one indeed.

Your new agent will receive more business and extra profits, so should be paying you some kind of franchise fee which will help to offset the costs of monitoring their progress. You will also need a carefully drafted contract which, among other things, will prevent your agents using your customer base to distribute competitors' goods.

Of course, this idea is not suitable for every company, but if a high proportion of your customers have small accounts, it is well worth serious consideration. It is not every company that will willingly give its customers away, even if doing so will save it money in the long run.

9 Measuring collection performance

The only way you are going to be able to gauge the success of your new credit control methods is to measure the individual performance of each credit controller and the amount of debt outstanding at the end of each month.

Measuring collectors' performance

It may be that you already operate some kind of system for comparing your collectors, probably based on the amount of cash each of them collects during the course of the month. But payment from a few large customers can distort this figure, and it is not a very reliable guide to the collector's performance.

You should now be setting up a *daily performance report* for each collector. This will serve the dual purpose of showing how effective each collector is, and also showing you how much cash is in transit, or promised, and when you can expect to receive it.

A suggested format for this report is shown in Figure 9.1. The report can be summarized every week, or every month if you prefer. The summary report is shown in Figure 9.2.

Each controller will probably fill in the following each day:

- The name and account number of each customer contacted
- Any payment promised by the customer, and when you should receive it
- Any payments received during the day.

This information should also appear on the customer contact and history form. At the end of the week, the controller fills in the number of calls made and the amount of cash received. This is then passed on to the supervisor or manager, who transfers the information to a weekly summary of all the collectors.

The only calls which are recorded are *contacts*, where the collector has been successful in speaking to the customer. The average collector should be able to manage 20–25 contacts per day. But there will also be a proportion of calls, possibly quite high, where the controller does not get through, and the recording of these calls should be left to the manager's discretion.

It is very important that you *use* the summary reports once they have been produced; otherwise your staff are simply wasting time completing them when they could be contacting more customers.

DAILY PERFORMANCE REPORT					
Credit Controller			Date		
Account no.	Customer name	Balance of account	Amount promised	Date promised	Date received

Figure 9.1 *Suggested format for daily performance report*

WEEKLY SUMMARY REPORT				
Date		Accounting period		
Credit controller	No. of calls	Amount promised	Amount received	Balance due this month
Totals				

Figure 9.2 *Suggested format for weekly summary report*

There is a very thin dividing line between collectors who are motivated because their performance is being monitored and they have targets to work towards each month, and collectors who are unhappy at the idea of wading through mountains of paperwork instead of doing the job they are supposed to. Make sure that they are not being asked for too much information and that the daily report does not become a painful ritual.

Make sure, too, that the report does not become a negative tool, used simply to spot those collectors who do not appear to be pulling their weight. Use it also to praise those who are being successful. You may want to award the most successful collector each month some kind of financial or material bonus – perhaps even a day off work.

If one collector does appear to be less successful than others, do not assume that it is necessarily his or her fault. He or she may be receiving a higher proportion of bad accounts than other collectors, or there may be other reasons which only he or she can tell you about. Whatever you do, do not issue rebukes in front of colleagues; speak to the collector privately and ask whether he or she can suggest any reasons why their performance has been below average.

Measuring debt

Here again, it is quite possible that you operate some kind of measuring system already. The most common is known as the *exhaust method.* Here the value of sales still outstanding at the end of each month is broken down by its age in days, weeks or months.

This method has the merit of being relatively simple, but it is not an accurate gauge of the success of your credit control. This is particularly true if your sales fluctuate a great deal between one part of the year and another. You may be in the ice-cream business, or perhaps a fireworks manufacturer. Here, increases or decreases in sales will lead to increases or decreases in the amount you collect and the resulting figures are close to meaningless.

Instead, you should be producing a *percentage debt report.* This method compares the aged debt balance remaining on the sales ledger each month with the actual sales totals for the same month. This then shows the *percentage* of the debt remaining uncollected.

Figure 9.3 shows how to produce this report; the figures are taken from a real company. If you have a PC and a spreadsheet package, this will make the task even simpler.

1 Arrange the monthly sales figures in chronological order down the first column.
2 Starting from the most recent month, arrange the aged balances diagonally so that the balance of the remaining debt each month appears on the same line as that month's sales figure. In this case, the one-month balance outstanding at the end of December (2,007) appears opposite the November sales figure (2,690) because November was the month in which the debt was created. The two-month balance at the end of December (1,774) is opposite the October sales figure (2,800). The three-month balance goes opposite the September sales figure (113), and so on.
3 Once the figures have been arranged in this way, it is a simple matter to calculate the percentage of sales uncollected at the end of each accounting period. For example, at the end of December, 74 per cent of November's sales remained uncollected

PERCENTAGE DEBT REPORT £'000's													
MONTH	SALES £	%	CURRENT £	%	MONTH 1 £	%	MONTH 2 £	%	MONTH 3 £	%	MONTH 4 £	%
JANUARY 1981	927	100	928	106	785	85	425	46	408	44	158	17
FEBRUARY 1981	1127	100	1094	97	798	71	523	46	358	32	164	15
MARCH 1981	1390	100	1312	94	767	70	475	34	372	27	207	14
APRIL 1981	1190	100	1146	96	826	69	585	49	336	28	131	11
MAY 1981	1340	100	1320	98	954	71	574	43	278	20	123	9
JUNE 1981	2017	100	2034	96	1331	63	792	37	358	16	145	6
JULY 1981	1671	100	1845	110	1435	85	782	46	357	21	150	8
AUGUST 1981	1458	100	1684	115	1209	82	591	40	304	20		
SEPTEMBER 1981	1940	100	2028	104	1343	69	661	34	113	5		
OCTOBER 1981	2800	100	2994	106	2405	85	1774	63				
NOVEMBER 1981	2690	100	2603	96	2007	74						
DECEMBER 1981	2765	100	2882	104								
AVERAGE		101.6										

Figure 9.3 *Format of a percentage debt report*

$$\frac{2007}{2690} \times 100$$

63 per cent of October's sales are uncollected

$$\frac{1774}{2800} \times 100$$

It is easy to see from this real-life example that customer accounts are not being followed up on a regular basis, and little regard is being given to the management and collection of the current month's invoices. Assuming the company operates monthly terms of trade, then there is very considerable room for improvement in these figures, and three-, four- and even five-month-old invoices should not be appearing on there at all.

In this particular case, much of the reason for the company's poor debt collection performance was the fact that their system for resolving customer queries was virtually non-existent. Three months after the systems and controls this book describes were introduced, the percentages had been reduced to 87 per cent for the current month, 51 per cent for month 1 and 35 per cent for month 2. Over £1.35 million came out of the sales ledger and into the company's bank account.

Of course, there will also be balances which are more than five months old. These have been ignored for the purposes of these figures. The older the invoices are, the harder they are to relate to a particular month's sale, and they represent hard-core debt which is going to take special measures to recover. In this company's case they were due mostly to a large backlog of long-forgotten and unresolved customer queries which took a special one-off effort to resolve.

Sometimes it is useful to average your performance over a period of several months. This is done in the bottom row of Figure 9.3. It involves totalling the aged balances and expressing them as a percentage of the total sales for the corresponding period.

10 Defining your credit policy

Every company should have a policy which lays down to whom it will grant credit, and under what circumstances. A sound, clearly defined policy will do the following for your company:

1 Minimize the amount of commercial risk you are exposed to.
2 Avoid bad debts, and thus reduce your collections costs and increase your turnover.
3 Ensure that your customers know exactly where they are with you, and therefore maintain the best possible relations with them.
4 Standardize practice throughout your company, especially if it is sited in more than one location.

If it does not already exist in written form, it should do. It should be the result of consultation with your managers, not an edict delivered from on high. Ideally, it should take the form of a manual to which anyone, credit controller or not, can easily refer. As well as stating your policy on granting credit it should describe what your company does to make sure your terms of trade are adhered to; this way, it will also serve as a manual for collections and sales staff who are new to the compnay.

As far as your customers are concerned, the important thing is that they should be *fully aware* of your credit policy. This applies particularly to new accounts. Customers should also be aware that you will not allow any deviations from the policy except in special circumstances and by written agreement with an appropriate member of staff. Again, the credit policy manual will lay down levels of authority within your company for granting exceptions to the rules. It should be made clear to the sales staff – and indeed to any other staff concerned – that no deviation will be permitted.

One way to produce this manual would be to divide it into three sections, as follows:

1 *General policy*	Your company's overall strategy for granting credit to customers, including your policy relating to new accounts and overdue ones. An outline for a general credit policy is described below.
2 *Credit control policy*	Detailed procedures for dealing with new customers, and telephone and postal collection of accounts. These have already been described in previous chapters.
3 *Query control*	This is treated separately in the following chapter.

General policy

Reservation of rights: Emphasize that it is not the right of any customer to *demand* credit. Credit should be granted only where the company sees fit, and you have a right to refuse or withdraw credit facilities at any time.

Who is authorized to give credit: You should clearly define a scale of authority for opening a new account, and lay down the criteria under which the person granting credit must refer the matter to higher authority. This may simply depend on the amount of credit you intend to give, with a scale beginning with the credit manager and moving upwards through the finance director to the managing director. You may also want to build in a risk factor to these levels of authority – for example, by saying that if the customer's bank reference is anything less than perfect it must be referred to the finance director.

How and where you state your terms of trade: The object here is to ensure that the customer can never use ignorance of these as an excuse for not paying. This is important: it has to stand up to a court of law if necessary. Describe, also, the procedure for making exceptions to these terms and who is authorized to do so.

Credit notes: A credit note is not simply an accounting procedure. To all intents and purposes, issuing one is the same as issuing a cheque. You therefore need a strict scale of authorization, and credit notes must never be authorized without sufficient written evidence that the issue is justified.

Suspension of credit facilities: From time to time it may be necessary to withdraw credit facilities from delinquent customers. The circumstances which would invoke such action, and by whom, should be clearly indicated within the body of the policy. The responsibilities for this action must be stated in a manner that leaves no room for confusion with either your own staff or the customer.

Action against bad debts: What would constitute a bad debt must be carefully explained. This will be closely related to the previous paragraph. This should not be confused with an overdue account. If your trading terms state payment is due 30 days from the date of invoice, at 31 days it is overdue. An invoice which is 30 days old – beyond the next statement date – can be considered a bad debt. At least, it should be viewed with caution, providing the normal collection procedures have been fully utilized. The action required to rectify a bad debt situation has to be clearly laid down in this policy, together with the authorization required to instigate such action.

Monitoring accounts: You should define who is responsible for maintaining your sales ledger debt, reporting on it to you and ensuring that customers do not pay late or exceed their credit limits.

The accounting period: This should also be defined in your credit policy document. Many companies work to a calendar monthly cycle, but some still use the old-fashioned lunar month so that two four-week months are followed by a five-week month. The calendar month system has only one disadvantage: some months have 30 days, others have 31. The lunar month has many drawbacks. It causes confusion within your company ('Is this a four- or five-week month?'); it confuses your customers, whose cut-off dates are unlikely to fit in easily with yours; and it distorts your collection figures because

NEW ACCOUNT APPLICATION FORM					
Name					
Address					
			Postcode		
Account address					
			Postcode		
Tel. Nos.		Tel. Nos.		Comp. Man A/C	
Man. Dir/Prop.			Ext.		
Fin. Dir/Acct.			Ext.		
Partners/Shareholders			Ext.		
			Ext.		
			Ext.		
Bght ledger supervisor					
A/C Inst.					
Bankers					
Trade ref. 1					
Trade ref. 2					
Annual T/O		Exp. credit limit		Audited A/Cs	
Subsidiaries					
Signed		Position		Date	
FOR INTERNAL USE					
Date recd		Representative		Initial Order	Y/N
Rep. report					
Ref. taken date		Received date		Ref. No.	
Credit limit agreed		A/C No.			
Credit controller			Date		
Approved by			Date		

Figure 10.1 *An example of a new account application form*

the longer the month, the more you will collect. A shorter month in your own company may fall prior to your customers' cut-off dates and accounts paid within the terms of trade could be defined as overdue.

New accounts: Who is responsible for ensuring that an application form is filled in and trade and banker's references are obtained, and how this is done (see Figure 10.1 for a sample form).

Credit limits: These should be regularly reviewed. A customer's financial standing may change for better or worse, or they may be wanting to buy more from you than previously. Inflation can also be a factor in your decision. Again, the decision needs to be taken by a properly authorized member of staff, and if the limit is to be increased you may want a new set of bank references.

Dealing with cash: How your customers' payments are to be handled so that they are credited as soon as possible. Who is responsible for banking and reporting cash receipts. If you are collecting cash from a very wide area, perhaps nationwide, could you gain by having the cash deposited in a local branch of your bank rather than being sent to your head office?

A credit policy manual is not a guide to getting rid of credit customers. It simply serves to ensure that your company takes no unnecessary risks when it delivers your products without collecting payment for them straightaway. Once everyone in the company has read it, there should be slightly less danger of KSCs managing director taking your credit manager out to lunch, cramming him or her full of champagne and caviare and getting him or her to sign an agreement to double KSC's credit limit just before they both slump over the table in an alcoholic stupor.

Above all, remember the adage: *a sale is not a sale until it has been paid for and the money is in the bank.*

11 Query control

As we saw with Trimmett and Co., who refused to pay any invoices until their complaint about £15.78 worth of eyebolts was resolved, one small query by a customer can lead to huge amounts of cash being unnecessarily tied up in your sales ledger.

You should, by now, have decreased the chances of a customer querying an invoice when, following your review, you removed the weaknesses in your company's functioning which could cause them. But we live in an imperfect world. If you are issuing invoices in any kind of large quantity, then sooner or later one of your customers will say:

'The arithmetic on this invoice is wrong. Could you issue another one please?'

'You've only supplied part of the goods we ordered, but you've charged us for the whole lot.'

'What do you mean, your invoice is overdue? You never sent us an invoice'.

Seventy-five per cent of these reasons for delays in payment are likely to be caused by the kind of minor administrative hitches that your company has in common with every other company. The remaining 25 per cent are using real or imagined queries as a pretext for not paying you. Whichever category a customer query falls into, *the onus is on you to resolve it.* Ultimately, you are the only person who will suffer if it is not resolved.

Almost any company of any size should have a *query control system.* This will allow you to:

(a) be aware of the value of payments being withheld due to problems with the goods or the invoices for them;
(b) know the weaknesses in your system which allow these problems to arise in the first place;
(c) know exactly what stage the resolution of each query has reached;
(d) ensure that the query is sorted out within a fixed period of time, and therefore that cash due to you is delayed for as short a time as possible.

You will probably want to formalize your query control system in your credit policy manual, but even if you do not, it should be there in black and white so that everyone in the company knows how it works.

Creating a query control system

First of all, *set a target time* for queries to be resolved. This will vary depending on the size and nature of your business, but in most cases five to seven days should be enough. The longer a complaint takes to be sorted out, the less chance there will be of an outcome satisfactory to both parties. Memories fade; paperwork gets lost. In extreme cases, the query remains outstanding for so long that the staff who were supposed to be dealing with it have left the company. There are no proper records of the query, so no-one knows whether or not it was genuine, and the invoice has to be written off.

Aim for simplicity. Time spent resolving queries is non-productive time. Your query control system must be simple to understand and to operate. It must not involve reams of paper being circulated to every staff member in quadruplicate every time a customer complains of being overcharged by 10p. If your system is not a simple one, it will end up causing more problems than it was intended to resolve.

Decide whose responsibility it is to be. Ideally, the system should be run by one person. It may even be a full-time job, at least if you have a large backlog of unresolved queries to start with. Inputting these queries into the new system will ensure that they are not overlooked, and will help you to classify them. They are likely to originate from the credit control department, because if you have followed the recommendations of this book it will be this department that produces most of the queries.

The system will involve three simple documents, examples of which are shown in Figures 11.1, 11.2 and 11.3. These are:

The query form	This serves as a record of the nature of the query and its resolution.
The query log	Records all queries that are in the system at any one time.

QUERY FORM						
Customer name			Account number			
Query type	Invoice total		Account total		Query no:	
Ageing	Current	1 Month	2 Months	3–5 Months	6–8 Months	9 Months +
TOTAL						
To			Invoice(s)			
From						
Date						
Query details						
Instructions/action required			Attachments		Yes	No
Completed by					Date	
Reply						
Further action required						
Completed by					Date	

Figure 11.1 *The query form*

QUERY LOG AND ANALYSIS						Period	From ________ To ________											
Date	Query No	Reply date	Action date	Customer detail	Account value	Query value	Query type											
							1	2	3	4	5	6	7	8	9	10	11	12

Figure 11.2 *The query log*

PROBLEM SUMMARY						Period						
Query Type	Outstanding at end of last period			Raised in current period			Resolved in current period			Query now outstanding		
	No:	A/C value	Query value	No:	A/C value	Query value	No:	A/C value	Query value	No:	A/C value	Query value
TOTALS												

Figure 11.3 *The query summary*

The query summary form A monthly analysis for management, showing the types of queries being received, how much money is involved, and how long it is taking to resolve them.

The Barnsley Fish-Boiling Company owe you £500. The invoice is due for payment in just over a week's time, and Arthur Beansprout phones them to make sure there won't be any problems in getting the cheque to you on time.

'Ah! glad you mentioned that, Mr Beansprout', says Mr Bottle in their bought ledger department. 'I've been meaning to ring you about that invoice. You've included VAT at 15 per cent, but the invoice is for inverse rectilinear scratchplates. I wouldn't swear to it, but I've got an idea inverse rectilinear scratchplates are zero-rated for VAT. Am I right?'

Arthur hasn't the faintest idea, but he says he'll check it out with your accounts department and let Mr Bottle know as soon as possible.

As soon as he has put the phone down, Arthur reaches for his pad of query forms. Each form has two copies of different colours underneath it, and the one he writes on is made of carbonless paper so he gets three copies of whatever he writes. The form itself is divided in half, with the space above the line for the details of the query, and the space below the line for a response from the appropriate department.

Arthur fills in BFBC's name and account number, and the number of the invoice in question. Then he writes: 'Invoice is for inverse rectilinear scratchplates. Customer thinks these should be zero-rated for VAT. Please could you check and, if he is right, issue a new invoice together with a credit note to cancel the incorrect invoice?'

As the date for resolution, he puts the 17th, which is five working days away. This should be more than enough time for the accounts department to sort out the query. He keeps the top copy for himself, and sends the other two to Doris Shrimpton, your recently-appointed query controller.

Her job is to enter the main details of Arthur's query in her query log. She gives it the next number in her sequence, and writes this on the form. In the box marked 'query type', she puts a '16'. This, she knows from her copy of the credit policy manual, stands for 'VAT query', and is used to analyse the nature of the query. If there are any supporting documents, such as invoices or delivery notes, that the person answering the query is going to need, she obtains a copy and attaches them. In this case, there are none, because the accounts department is responsible for responding to the query and they will have a copy of the invoice.

Next, Mrs Shrimpton sends a postcard to BFBC to acknowledge the fact that you know about their query and it is being dealt with (See Figure 11.4). It also tells them the query reference number to quote if they ring up about it again. It has her name clearly printed at the bottom, so that if they do phone up, they know who is responsible for sorting out the problem.

Mrs Shrimpton keeps one copy of the query form for her own file, and sends the last copy to Mrs Dork in the accounts department. Mrs Dork checks her booklet on VAT rates and finds that, yes, inverse rectilinear scratchplates are indeed zero-rated. She types out an invoice with the correct amount on it, and sends it off by first-class post to BFBC, with a compliments slip apologizing for the error, and at the same time forwarding a credit note for the first invoice. Then she writes on the query form: 'Customer is correct. Revised invoice and credit note sent today.' She signs and dates the form, and returns it to Doris Shrimpton.

Doris Shrimpton records the query in her log as having been resolved. She forwards a copy of the form to Arthur, who can then make a note on his customer history form that the new invoice has gone out. He may also need to telephone BFBC to tell them this.

The whole process has taken only a day and a half from query to resolution, and the new invoice will be with BFBC in time for them to process it and still have a cheque on its way to you at the correct time. They will also have the credit note, which should forestall any difficulty in settling the account.

TO: (COMPANY NAME)

FROM

Your ref:

Dear

We acknowledge your query of the .... and confirm that this matter has been passed to the appropriate department with a request that they give it their immediate attention.

If you should require any further information please feel free to write or telephone, quoting our reference number Q/........

Yours sincerely,

QUERY CONTROLLER

Figure 11.4 *Postcard to customer*

Things will not always run as smoothly as this, of course. The accounts department have a number of query forms in their 'In' tray and it is possible they may take longer than the specified five days to get round to answering them. In this case, it is part of Doris Shrimpton's responsibilities as query controller to send them a written reminder (see Figure 11.5). If they are really slow in replying, they may need a second reminder (see Figure 11.6), or the delay might even have to be reported to a senior manager if it gets totally out of hand. But although Mrs Dork in the accounts department can be a bit slow off the mark sometimes, she always gets things done sooner rather than later.

Finally, Doris Shrimpton fills in a query summary immediately after each month-end. This contains the information that you or your managers need to know about customer queries for that month. It includes such items as:

- The number of queries and complaints which arose during the month; how many were resolved, and how many were carried forward into the following month;
- the total value of the accounts involved;
- an analysis of queries by type, so that, for example, if it emerged that too many invoices were going out with wrongly calculated VAT figures, someone could sit down with the accounts department and make sure they were properly trained in how VAT works;
- comparative data for previous months, so that you can see trends rather than a set of numbers in isolation;
- a list of queries which are still outstanding because they have not been resolved within the specified time, and the reasons why.

MEMORANDUM

TO:

FROM: QUERY CONTROLLER

DATE:

RE: OUTSTANDING CUSTOMER QUERIES:
FIRST REMINDER

The attached query/queries have now been outstanding for more than five working days.

Please would you ensure that they are resolved immediately or, alternatively, please advise me in writing of the reason for the delay and when you expect the queries to be resolved.

Thank you.

QUERY CONTROLLER

cc. Credit Control Manager

Figure 11.5 *First query reminder*

MEMORANDUM

TO:

FROM: QUERY CONTROLLER

DATE:

RE: OUTSTANDING CUSTOMER QUERIES:
SECONDREMINDER

A FURTHER FIVE DAYS HAVE NOW PASSED SINCE OUR FIRST REMINDER, DATED............REGARDING THE ATTACHED COPY QUERY/QUERIES.

IT IS IMPERATIVE THAT YOU RESOLVE THIS MATTER AND RETURN THE QUERY FORM IMMEDIATELY. ALTERNATIVELY, MAY I PLEASE HAVE YOUR COMMENTS BY RETURN.

QUERY CONTROLLER

cc. Credit Control Manager

Figure 11.6 *Second query reminder*

Sometimes it is tempting to bypass the query control system. If he were so minded, Arthur Beansprout himself could have rung the accounts department to find out what the situation was and to ask them to provide a new invoice if necessary. But once this has been allowed to happen on a single occasion, it can easily turn into a habit and the whole purpose of the system will have been defeated.

Your staff should not be regarding your query control system as simply an additional piece of red tape designed to fill any hours of leisure they may have between 9 a.m. and 5 p.m. If its purpose and benefits have been explained to them properly, they can only react positively to it.

A simple, effective query control system not only speeds customers' complaints and queries (and therefore their payment of your bills) it also places your middle management that much closer to the marketplace. They know more about how customers are reacting to your products and the way you charge for them, and they have a greater awareness of your customers' needs. Your customers are happier, because they know that, it you do make a mistake, you can be relied upon to put it right as quickly as possible.

12 Collecting money from overseas customers

The changes we have described so far relate mainly to companies dealing with customers in Britain. If you have ever been involved in the export market, you will know that the problems involved in collecting money are much the same, but it takes longer.

If you are in a situation where your products and services are now beginning to sell increasingly to overseas customers, you will have found that, in most cases, you have to extend your trading terms. In some cases, they have to be extended so far that cash flow problems can result. You can overcome the situation by borrowing money, but this can harm your future profitability. Although exporting will increase your sales, its net effect on your balance sheet may be negative if you are unable to finance it yourself.

You should be operating the same procedures for foreign customers as for those in Britain – contacting them before the money is due, establishing a record of their payment history and including them in your query control system. But some of your methods will need adapting for export customers.

For example, Arthur Beansprout needs to think very hard before he picks up the telephone to chase an overdue cheque from Borneo. The cost of the call may be more than the value of the invoice. The time difference may mean the customer is fast asleep in bed just when Arthur is debating whether to have cheese or egg mayonnaise sandwiches at lunchtime. The customer may speak a variety of tribal dialects, but not a word of English. In any of these cases, it might be more sensible to use the telex or the fax machine to chase that invoice – provided they have fax machines in Borneo, of course.

Although you will probably have to extend the period of credit you give, this may work to your advantage since it affords you more time to resolve any queries raised by the customer before the invoice becomes due for payment. There are fewer reasons and excuses for late payment when the customer has six weeks to pay instead of four.

The method of payment is more important, as well. Your payment terms should specify that the account is to be paid to a British location and in sterling. This avoids delays in transferring payments to Britain; it means there are fewer additional costs to be faced, and that you are not subject to fluctuations in exchange rates.

Many customers will neither be able nor willing to go along with this. In a case where the customer will only pay in local currency, the pricing of your goods or services must reflect these extra costs. Alternatively, you may wish to reconsider your decision to export your products there in the first place.

There are various financial aids to security in the export market. If you are dealing with a politically or financially unstable country, you should insist on confirmed letters of credit. You may wish to use bills of exchange. These can be drawn either on sight or, if you are granting extended credit, at a fixed number of days after sight. The Export Credits Guarantee Department or trade insurance companies can be useful and can assist you to accept accounts which represent a big risk. However, these are outside the scope of this book, and your bank manager is the person to talk to about them.

You also need to use more stringent new-account procedures for foreign customers, and to monitor accounts and their credit limits more frequently. You may not have easy access to their annual accounts, as many countries (including the USA) do not require companies to register them. Local clearing banks (possibly via their branches in London, if any) can be a useful alternative source of information. Your own experience is always the best guide. Correct use of the customer history form and close liaison with the export sales department are essential.

However many precautions you take before you start dealing with an overseas customer you are involving yourself in a higher degree of risk than when selling to someone in Britain. Equally, though, the rewards from the increased market can be much greater. In general, there is no reason why most of the methods described in previous chapters of this book should not be just as effective when applied to companies abroad.

13 Where do I go from here?

At this stage, it is very easy to put your feet up on your desk, breathe a sigh of satisfaction and take the rest of the day off. You have completely transformed the way your company functions; it now runs smoothly and efficiently and the cash is coming in by the lorryload every morning.

Of course, it's not going to be like that. If you did have a hard core of sales ledger debt which has now been turned into cash, your bank statement is going to look a lot healthier than it has done for some time. You may have reduced your average debt from 55 days to 35 days outstanding without any gargantuan effort on the part of your credit controllers. But getting that figure down to, say, 30 days will take a very great deal of effort because there is now less cash available to be wrung out of the ledger.

Your company is now going to need some strong management. As the receipts dwindle after a few months, there will be a tendency to think that your new methods are failing. This will be especially true if people were halfhearted about them in the first place. It is up to you to keep the momentum going now before things start to flag and people start creeping back into their old habits. You should constantly be reviewing collection targets to ensure that they are realistic in view of the decline in collections, and yet sufficiently demanding to keep people motivated. You should be actively using the reports your collections staff give you, and you should also be seen to be using them.

Assuming that you are able to keep this momentum going, there are other pieces of fine-tuning you could employ to extract that extra couple of percentage points improvement. Again, these will only be cost-effective with the larger accounts – the 20 per cent of customers that owe you 80 per cent of the money.

Monthly cheque runs: Many of the accounts will agree to someone collecting their cheques in person on the day they produce them each month. This means a member of your staff preparing a route to collect a number of high-value cheques all in one day, and either banking them locally where they are collected, or in your own local branch before they close.

One large company sent out an employee very early in the morning so that he arrived on the first customer's doorstep at 9 a.m. He then travelled to Manchester, Leeds and Nottingham, collecting five or six cheques on route. The cheques totalled over £1½ million. If they had been posted, they would have taken two or three days to be credited. The interest on a sum of this magnitude for three days, collected twelve times a year, adds up to a very considerable amount. At certain times of the year, such as Christmas and Easter, when mail is idle in your postbox for several days, this saving can be even greater.

Reminders: Provided he is tactful about it, Arthur Beansprout could also ring up customers with large balances on the eve of their cheque run and give them another reminder. This way he will ensure that all the invoices due are being paid, and also that there are no problems which might delay your cheque. If there is a problem, and the cheques are machine-produced, Arthur could ask for a handwritten one instead. Without this reminder, it will be at least two or three days before he becomes aware of any delays, and by the time the cheque arrives it may be too late for your month-end. Not only does this affect your collection performance, it also loses you interest.

Other special cheque requests: Now that your service to them has improved so dramatically, your major customers may well have sufficient reserves of bonhomie to give you a special cheque before their normal cheque run if they owe you a large sum of money. If not, they may still respond to some of the white lies suggested for collecting money from difficult customers in Chapter 7 (though, of course, they are not difficult customers!)

Special attention for customer queries: If a customer has a large invoice about to become due for payment, and also has a query or complaint which is likely to delay the payment until after your cut-off date, Arthur might be able tactfully to harass the department dealing with the query into resolving it earlier than they normally would have done.

Bank transfers: Bank transfers are becoming a much more widespread means of remitting payments between companies. They have the obvious advantage of saving the two or three days a cheque would take in transit, and having to wait for clearance. The Clearing House Automated Payment System (CHAPS) will transfer payment to your account within hours in the case of a branch-to-branch transfer (e.g. Barclays to Barclays) or half a day if different banks are involved. The minimum amount that can be transferred was recently reduced from £10,000 to £5,000. The main problem with this method of transfer is the set fee of £12.00, charged to your customer. All that is required to initiate payment by this system is for your customer to give his bank written instructions, which must include your name, the amount, and your banker's name, address and sorting code number, and your account number. Clearly this is a much easier and quicker way to have your accounts paid than the conventional posting of a cheque – not to mention the additional interest you will be earning or saving.

Larger invoices: Where an exceptionally large invoice is produced in any one month, Arthur could be given a copy before it is sent to the customer. He would then be in a position to check that it was being processed and that no queries were likely to arise. Payment would therefore be possible even before details of that particular invoice registered on your sales ledger.

Special clearance: It is often possible to obtain special rapid clearance of a cheque on payment of a fee.

There are probably other ways of squeezing extra money out of your sales ledger that we have not mentioned here. Use a little lateral thinking: get round the table with anyone – from senior management to mailroom clerks – and ask for ideas. Look at what happens as your month-end approaches and ask yourself whether there is any way of speeding up the process of getting money to the bank.

Here, as in every previous chapter of this book, there is endless room for *creativity*. None of the suggestions made here is meant to be followed slavishly; nor does the book make any claim to comprehensiveness. The idea throughout is to get you thinking about the way *your company* collects its cash. Your company is unique, and some of the solutions to your company's problems will be unique as well.

Turning invoices into cheques does not require any particular magical ability, like turning loaves into fishes or water into wine. Anyone can do it, given the right investment in time, money and training. It is one of the best investments you can make, for it is the launching pad for your company's success. Every pound of tied-up cash that you can release from its fetters will ultimately be reflected in the bottom line of your balance sheet.

But what of the future? Arthur and his colleagues have undergone complete transformation, not only in the manner that they approach your customers, but in learning new methods of operation. This type of exercise is never easy, and they should be congratulated for their achievements.

Most important of all is that their thinking patterns will also have changed. No longer will they simply go on from day to day, without any thought about how they perform, or about the consequences of their actions on the company's profitability and its relations with its customers. They will now be continually searching for ways of improving not only their own working day, but their future and that of the company.

Where should Arthur be looking for those additional improvements? Computerization is an obvious area. New and better equipment and software are constantly coming on to the market. Paperless invoicing is already with us (albeit on a very limited scale) but as the power of the microchip increases, and more and more computers become capable of talking to each other, it may not be long before this system is within reach of even the smallest firms.

Before this method of ordering, invoicing and accepting payment can be installed widely, all businesses must undertake a vigorous review of their operations. If the wrong price, for example, is transmitted between computers the invoice will be automatically rejected by the receiving computer, and the problems this creates in re-establishing the validity of the invoice are far worse than with any existing system.

Paperless invoicing allows your customer to instruct his computer to place an order for your goods direct with your own computer. Your computer will automatically process that order, picking out the items ordered from your store with the aid of a robot, and having them packed and sent to your dispatch department together with a delivery note. Your computer then automatically advises your customer's computer of dispatch, and invoices direct into your customer's computer which adjusts its stock record and transfers payment to your bank account.

Whatever Arthur and his colleagues do today to improve their collection performance, there is always going to be a more efficient way tomorrow, so they need to undertake a ceaseless search for improvement.

Appendix A
How to carry out your review

This Appendix covers the following:

- Which areas to look at in your review of the way your company works
- How to produce a report on the review
- How to act on the review

Appendix B includes a sample questionnaire which you may wish to use as the framework for your review.

The contents of both Appendices as a whole will almost certainly need to be adapted to the structure of your own particular company. For example, the separate functions of the sales and accounts departments, as we have described them here, may overlap in your company.

As we stressed in Chapter 2, the review should cover *every* department whose function could have a bearing on the way your company issues invoices and collects payment for them.

The sales and/or marketing department

There are six main aspects of the department's work to be reviewed.

1 *Documents:* The paperwork your customer receives from you – does it clearly set out the terms on which you and the customer are trading?
2 *Discounts:* Is your company obtaining a tangible benefit by offering discounts to customers?
3 *Order processing:* Are your customers getting the goods they want at the time they want them?
4 *Invoices and statements:* Do they clearly show how much the goods cost and when and how they are to be paid for? Are they being sent out promptly or do they spend weeks gathering dust in someone's 'Pending' tray?
5 *Queries:* Are queries and complaints from customers being handled promptly and courteously?
6 *New accounts:* Are you making a balanced and well informed decision about who gets credit and who does not?

Let us look at these six items in more detail.

Documents

The terms on which you and the customer are trading should be clearly stated on every piece of paper your customer receives from you. These would normally include:

- Price lists
- Brochures
- Dispatch notes
- Invoices
- Monthly statements
- Reminders about overdue amounts

Don't use small print to describe your terms of trade, and don't place this information on the back of the document where it will not be read.

Be consistent. Don't print different payment terms on different documents. Either the customer will be confused, or they will exploit the inconsistency to their own advantage by taking longer to pay. Printing the same terms on all of your company's stationery will also avoid any misunderstandings by customers who are dealing with more than one of your locations simultaneously.

If you correct simple errors such as these, you are removing another excuse from the customer's armoury. Remember, credit is *not* their automatic right: you should grant it only when and where you feel it will not be misused.

Discounts

Customer discounts are often a necessity if you are to compete with the rest of the market, but equally often they are granted to customers when they need not be. Generally speaking, *if you can get away with not offering a discount for early or prompt payment, then don't offer one.* Discounts are an expensive marketing tool: rarely does the benefit of having the cash early outweigh the cost of granting the customer 5 or 10 per cent off the price of the goods. Also, discounts are very widely abused: customers will pay late but still deduct the discount from their payment, with little or no action being taken to recover the wrongly deducted discount.

Order processing

Ask yourself these questions. *Is each new order being processed and sent off to the customer as quickly as it could be?* Likewise, if you cannot fulfil all or part of the order, is the customer being told this? What action do you intend to take, or how should the customer go about re-ordering? It is very bad customer relations to leave the customer in ignorance until after the goods have been delivered of the fact that you cannot supply all of them. If the order is sent off incomplete, does the person doing the invoicing know, so that the missing items are not charged for by mistake? These could all give your customer justification in delaying payment.

Invoices and statements

How and when do you produce your invoices? Do they go out with the order, or two weeks later when somebody gets around to typing them out?

Do you give priority to larger invoices? This might include sending them by first-class post or even by courier if it means you will catch your customer's cut-off date for paying invoices. Many companies pay all their invoices for the previous month at the beginning of the following month, so you might have to wait only a week to get paid instead of a month. It can also avoid your invoices arriving on your customer's premises too late to be paid within the period you want, and therefore becoming overdue through no fault of the customer. It is in the area of invoicing that *knowing how your customer works* is most important.

Are your *statements,* if any, going out to the customer as soon as possible after the end of the month? Are they being checked, and reconciled to invoices if necessary, or are they simply being stuffed into envelopes and posted?

Queries

If you drag your feet when it comes to sorting out queries from your customers, it is you that suffers. More often than not, they can take their custom elsewhere if they are not happy with the service you are providing. And time taken to resolve problems with goods or invoices means delays in your receiving payment.

Looking at how customer queries and complaints are resolved is one of the most important areas for your review. The likelihood is that you do not operate any kind of control system which monitors the progress of queries from their point of origin to when they have been sorted out and the goods paid for. Your review should include a detailed analysis of all queries you have received over at least six months. This will give you two important pieces of information.

(a) What are the underlying problems in the company which are causing these queries to be raised in the first place?
(b) What effect are these queries having on the amount of cash you collect, and how much revenue are you losing as a result?

If, as a result of your review, you can prevent queries arising in the first place, the review will have been a success. Again, the motto you should have writ large above your desk is 'Prevention is better than cure'.

Chapter 11 describes a simple, effective system for monitoring the progress of queries.

New accounts

Here, we are assuming that it is the responsibility of your sales and/or marketing departments to provide the information required for a decision whether or not a customer is to be given an account. The principal question to be answered is *does your Credit Manager have sufficient information to make a balanced decision?*

Does the customer have to fill in an application form to obtain credit from you? If not, would it be worthwhile to introduce a form?

Do you take references from the customer's bank and from other people the customer does business with? Do you ask for a copy of their audited accounts, and if so how much reliance do you place on them? Bear in mind that the information these contain is usually at least a year out of date; they are really only of use in conjunction with a report from someone who has actually been out and seen the customer on their own premises to acquire a feel for the way they do business.

Are you granting manageable credit limits to new customers? This may not always be appropriate if you have a long-standing customer who gives you large amounts of business and whom experience has shown to be financially sound. In any case, where you have any doubts whatsoever about their ability to pay, it is worth imposing a credit limit.

Is the decision to give credit being made by a person with suitable authority? You may wish to centralize all decision-making in one person, perhaps the credit manager, or you may have a hierarchy depending on the amount of credit to be granted.

See Chapter 10 for more detailed information on the granting of new accounts, and a suggested design for a credit application form.

Your Sales and Marketing departments are the front-end of the process of granting credit: it is they who first introduce the new customers, and they (in consultation with the credit manager) who assess their suitability for being given credit. Their duties do not stop there, of course: they are the main link between yourself and your customers and they have a major responsibility for making sure the customer is kept happy. But the job of monitoring exactly who owes you how much is that of the accounts or finance department, and they should be the next target of your review.

The accounts and/or finance department

What is being done to keep sales ledger debt to a minimum? Does your accounts department simply chase it up on an ad hoc basis, or do you have a proper system to deal with it? Of course, the size or nature of your company may make the former option the more sensible.

And if you do operate a proper system of credit control, is it effective? Are the letters you send out likely to get positive results, or are they a waste of a postage stamp? If you telephone people, are you getting value for money from the call?

And perhaps most importantly, *do you, the manager, know who owes you how much?* If you do not already receive one on a regular basis, your review should include a sales ledger analysis. This will allow you to work out how much money is needlessly tied up in your sales ledger when it could be appearing on the credit side of your bank statement. Make sure, too, that reports you get are telling you what you need to know to run the company, rather than being part of a ritual which is only marginally more meaningful than counting paperclips.

Rather than looking at one month in isolation, take at least six months' worth of month-end sales ledger balances as a percentage of sales. Your analysis will show whether your performance is improving, deteriorating or simply fluctuating at random. But it is no use knowing this information and not acting on it, so *set yourself a target.* Say to yourself something along these lines: 'By December, I will decrease my sales ledger debt by 25 per cent.' Your current month will normally show 100 per cent of your debt still outstanding, and this figure will reduce proportionally in previous months, so you need to take an average figure for the period you are looking at.

See Chapter 9 for ideas and suggestions on the production of a regular sales ledger analysis.

Other departments

Your sales and accounting departments are probably going to receive the most detailed scrutiny during your review, but eventually just about everyone in the company is going to come under the microscope. You are going to need to look at the following:

- Your *production department,* if it looks as though invoices are not being paid because your goods are faulty, badly designed or not what the customer wants.
- Your *distribution department,* if shortfalls or breakages are the reason why your customers are not paying.
- Your *service department,* if you are giving any form of after-sales service. This department will often be more geared towards getting the job done than making sure your company gets paid for it.

Finally, you need to look at the way the *lines of communication* work within your company. If Mr Patel in the accounts department knows that your best customer, Deadloss Ltd., is £5,000 over its credit limit and on the verge of bankruptcy, would he think of passing the information on to Mrs Crump in the sales department so that your company puts a stop on the account? Or, conversely, if another customer tells Mrs Crump that she has sent them the wrong size of widget, will Mr Patel ever get to hear about it so that the customer doesn't get a nasty letter when the invoice becomes overdue?

Producing a report on your review

The end result of this review should be a report setting out the reviewer's findings on each department. It should list both strengths and weaknesses, and it should propose solutions where there is room for improvement.

The report should not beat about the bush: if failings by one particular department are causing log-jams in the rest of the system, it should say so. Equally, though, it should give credit where credit is due. If Mr Wilkins, the credit control assistant, suggests that reminder letters should have the word URGENT stamped in red on the envelope, then the report should give him credit for the idea. Even if the result of the review is quite unfavourable, the report should not come across as a swingeing indictment of bureaucratic bungling.

Act on the report, and *make it a democratic exercise.* You should regard it as a consultation document for everyone in a position of responsibility who is affected by its findings, not as a management report for your eyes only. Get round the table with the people concerned and ask them for their recommendations. Once these have been agreed, make sure a final report is produced to incorporate them. You may wish this to take the form of a permanent *credit policy document,* which sets down the company's strategy concerning granting credit in the first place, and then making sure your customers adhere to your terms of trade.

Make sure that everyone knows what their responsibilities are in implementing the recommendations. And finally, *follow the matter up.* Once everyone has had reasonable time to change the way they go about doing things, sit down with them again and check how they are progressing. Only in this way will you ensure that the company has not slipped back into its old, bad habits six months later and that all this hard work has not gone to waste.

Appendix B Sample questionnaire

This questionnaire is based on one in actual use by the author in his capacity as a management consultant. It covers all the main areas a consultant would ask before embarking on a review of your company. *It is not a checklist:* just because you answer 'no' to a question does not imply that your company is deficient in any way. The purpose of the questionnaire is to help you orgainize your thoughts. It covers the following:

1 *People:* who is managing the company, and what experience they have.
2 *The market:* who you are competing with, and what is your position in the field.
3 *Your terms of trade:* whom you grant credit to, and how much.

4 *Your sales/marketing departments:* how you price and sell your products.
5 *Accounting:* how your sales ledger, invoicing and statement systems work.
6 *Credit control:* how you collect your debts.
7 *Personnel:* how many you have; their strengths and weaknesses.
8 *General:* overall impressions of morale and efficiency in the company.

THE QUESTIONNAIRE

SECTION 1

SENIOR MANAGEMENT

(a) Give full names and qualifications of the following, and state how long each has been in this position:

- (i) Senior Management Accountant
- (ii) Senior Finance/Treasury Accountant
- (iii) Credit Manager
- (iv) Sales Manager
- (v) Production Manager
- (vi) Transport Manager
- (vii) Personnel Manager
- (viii) Administration Manager
- (ix) DP Manager
- (x) Other key personnel and departmental supervisors, giving correct title and function

(b) If any of the above have been in their respective positions for less then six months, give their previous commercial background.

SECTION 2

BUSINESS ACTIVITIES

(a) Full description of UK business activities
(b) Full description of export business activities
(c) Does the company have a monopoly or near-monopoly?
- (i) In the UK
- (ii) In the rest of the world

(d) If not, how much competition does it have?
 (i) Strong
 (ii) Medium
 (iii) Poor
(e) Who are the top three competing companies?
(f) How does the company compare with its competitors for
 (i) Price
 (ii) Delivery
 (iii) Service
 (iv) Quality?
(g) Are its products/services
 (i) Repetitive
 (ii) One-off sales
 (iii) Long-term repetitive (i.e. more than twelve months between sales)?

SECTION 3

TERMS OF TRADE

(a) What are the company's normal terms of trade?
(b) Does it have specific variations to its terms of trade for
 (i) Particular customers?
 (ii) Particular product ranges?
(c) How do these terms of trade compare with those of competitors (give examples)?
(d) How many customers enjoy
 (i) Extended credit facilities
 (ii) Contract terms?
(e) Who are they, and what are the reasons for the extension of credit in each case?
(f) Who makes the decision on granting of extended credit or contract terms?
(g) Obtain samples of extended credit facility confirmation letters, contracts etc.

SECTION 4

SALES AND MARKETING

I. Distribution methods

(a) Are products/services sold direct to the user or through a wholesaler or other third party?
(b) If both apply, in what proportions and what criteria decide which method is used?
(c) Are the products/services of a seasonal nature?
(d) Are the customers and/or end users affected by seasonal influences?
(e) Are the products/services franchised? If so, obtain copies of contracts or agreements

II. Sales force

(a) Is there a sales force?
(b) How many sales staff/representatives are employed?
(c) Does each have a specific area to cover?
(d) What is the percentage personnel turnover per annum?
(e) Do representatives work to a fixed cycle of customer visits?
(f) What criteria are used to decide who the sales staff visit and how often?
(g) Is the sales force at full strength?
(h) If not, which areas are not being worked?
(i) How many calls are needed to obtain an order?
(j) Cost per call:
(k) Cost per order:
(l) Who does the sales force report to? Give full details of key management
(m) Is the sales force involved in collecting accounts?

(n) How are they paid?
  (i) Salary levels
  (ii) Commission
  (iii) Allowances
  (iv) Expenses
  (v) Company car
  (vi) Incentives
  (vii) Other
(o) When is commission paid: when the sale is made, or when it is paid for?
(p) Is commission deducted for unpaid accounts?
(q) Obtain samples of any relevant sales reports, etc.

III Sales offices

(a) How many sales offices are there, and where?
(b) Explain the function of each office and its staffing
(c) Which, if any, produce
  (i) Invoices?
  (ii) Credit notes?
(d) Obtain samples of each
(e) Where are their permanent records stored?

IV Pricing and discounts

(a) Profit before tax as a percentage of turnover
  (i) In total
  (ii) For each product line
(b) Are any discounts granted on sales?
(c) If so, what criteria are used and who qualifies?
(d) Who makes the decision as to whether a discount is granted?

V Order processing

(a) How many orders per day
  (i) At Head Office: direct and via sales force
  (ii) At sales offices: direct and via sales force
(b) Are the company's sales on target for the year?
(c) If not, give reasons for the shortfall or excess
(d) How are credits actioned?
(e) How long from when the order is received to when the customer receives an acknowledgement?
(f) How long from when the order is received to when the customer receives the goods?
(g) Do some products take longer than others to deliver?
(h) If so, what are they, and how much longer do they take?
(i) What proportion of sales do they represent?
(j) Are part deliveries made?
(k) If so, is each part delivery invoiced separately?
(l) Does delivery involve installing goods or products?
(m) If so, does the customer sign a satisfaction note?
(n) When does invoicing occur
  (i) on installed orders?
  (ii) on other orders?
(o) Is payment ever made in stages?
(p) If so, at what intervals and over what period?
(q) Are retentions involved?
(r) If so, for how long and what percentage?

VI Customers

(a) How many new accounts are opened each month?
(b) How many customers pay cash and how many are granted credit?

(c) What procedure is used for dealing with new accounts by
  (i) Sales staff
  (ii) Sales office
  (iii) Credit Control?
(d) What references are required (e.g. bank, trade, agency)
(e) Are annual accounts requested?
(f) Is the first order held until the details are checked?
(g) Is there a limit on the value of the first order?
(h) Is a credit limit fixed?
(i) How often are credit limits reviewed, and how?
(j) Who is responsible for carrying out the review?

VII Distribution

(a) How are goods distributed:
  (i) Own transport
  (ii) Outside carriers (road or rail: state which)
  (iii) Post
  (iv) Combination of the above?
(b) What is the average time for delivery?
(c) Is the invoice sent before or after the goods, or at the same time?
  How long?
(d) Are returnable chargeable containers involved?
(e) Is confirmation of delivery obtained?
(f) If so, where is it kept?

VIII Servicing

(a) Are servicing calls made?
(b) If so, under what circumstances?
(c) How often are they made?

(d) Would they be requested by the customer?
(e) What is the time delay in actioning (d)?
(f) Is there a service contract?
(g) If so, is it annual, quarterly or monthly?
(h) What does a service call cost, and how is it costed?
(i) Obtain copies of typical service contracts
(j) Are additional charges made over and above the normal contract charge?
(k) If so, what criteria are used to define whether a service call is charged or covered by the contract?
(l) Are service calls made by the sales force, or is there a separate force of service engineers?

SECTION 5

SALES ACCOUNTING

I. Methods and equipment

(a) Give a full description of the company's sales accounting methods
(b) What equipment is used?
(c) How long has the present system been in use?
(d) If less than three years, what were previous methods and equipment?
(e) Full description of all printouts and other documentation produced weekly, monthly and quarterly
(f) Does the equipment function adequately?
(g) How often does it break down, and how long does it take to be serviced?

II Invoicing

(a) Describe documents used to prepare invoices (obtain samples)
(b) Who prepares these documents?
(c) How long between receipt of these documents and preparation of the invoice?
(d) Who prepares the invoices?
(e) Obtain a sample invoice and describe how each part works if not immediately obvious.
(f) Are invoices prepared daily or batched?
(g) Are invoices forward- or back-dated?
(h) Are they sent first-class post?
(i) Where are the invoice copies stored, and how?
(j) Can extra copies be obtained if necessary?

III Credit notes

(a) Describe documents used to prepare credit notes (obtain samples)
(b) Who prepares these documents?
(c) How long between receipt of these documents and preparation of the credit note?
(d) Who prepares the credit notes?
(e) Obtain a sample credit note and describe how each part works if not immediately obvious.
(f) Are credit notes prepared daily or batched?
(g) Are credit notes forward- or back-dated?
(h) Are they sent first-class post?
(i) Where are the credit note copies stored, and how?
(j) Can extra copies be obtained if necessary?
(k) What are the limits of authority for the issue of credit notes?
(l) Is the wages department advised when there is a chargeback of commission due because of a credit note?

IV Statements

(a) What is the average period required to produce statements after the cut-off date?
(b) Where are statements produced?
(c) What is the average length of time taken to post statements?
(d) Are they sent by first-class post?
(e) Do they include a remittance advice section?
(f) If so, what percentage are used by customers?
(g) Are statements produced on an
  (i) Open item
  (ii) Balance forward
  (iii) Other basis?
(h) If there is a brought forward balance, is it analysed on the statement?
(i) Are statements sent before or after they have been balanced to the sales ledger control account?
(j) Are they produced singly or with copies?
(k) What are the copies used for, and where are they held?
(l) If there is a credit balance on an account, will a statement still be prepared and sent?
(m) What percentage of statements are returned undelivered (e.g. gone away, not known)?
(n) When this happens, what procedure is followed?
(o) Obtain samples of statements.

V The sales ledger

(a) What form does it take (e.g. printout, card)?
(b) Is it indexed
  (i) Alphabetically
  (ii) By account number
  (iii) Geographically
  (iv) Other method (specify)

(c) Who posts entries to the ledger?
(d) Are these entries posted daily or batched?
(e) How many credit balances are there, and what is their value?
(f) Why do credit balances exist?
(g) How are short payments handled (e.g. journal entries)?
(h) Who makes journal entries, and how many are there?
(i) Are journal entries made daily, or batched?
(j) Are all accounts reconciled at present?
(k) Are they regularly reconciled?
(l) How many are not reconciled, and why?
(m) How long have they been unreconciled and what is their value?
(n) How are customers' debit notes handled?

VI Receipts

(a) How is incoming cash handled, and who opens the mail?
(b) To whom are payments distributed?
(c) How many times per day are payments received?
(d) Are remittance advices, if any, attached to the payments?
(e) Who ultimately receives the payments?
(f) Are they entered in a cash book, and if so how?
(g) How often are payments made into the bank?
(h) Who prepares the bank paying-in book?
(i) At what stage are details of payments made passed to the sales ledger, if this is done manually?
(j) What documents, if any, are used to input details into the sales ledger (e.g. copy cash sheet)?
(k) Are payments allocated to the respective accounts daily, or are they batched?
(l) Does allocation always take place before cash is posted to the ledger?

(m) Who allocates cash, and is it up to date? If not, what is the backlog?
(n) Under what circumstances is cash not allocated?
(o) What happens to cash that cannot be allocated?
(p) How many payments are accompanied by:
- company remittance advice
- customer's own remittance advice?

(q) When are payments posted, and is there a backlog?
(r) How are non-cash receipts (e.g. credit transfers, standing orders, direct debits etc.) handled?
(s) How often does the bank advise the company of these receipts?

VII Credit control/Sales ledger personnel

(a) Full names, initials and qualifications of all personnel with description of function
(b) Length of service with company – If less than six months, previous commercial background?
(c) What is staff establishment?
(d) Is department at full strength?
(e) If not, give reasons
(f) Is establishment adequate to handle workload?

VIII General

(a) What is the basis of the accounting calendar?
(b) Is the cut-off date for invoice posting the same as that for cash posting?
(c) If not, specify the difference and the reason
(d) When does the financial year end?

SECTION 6

CREDIT CONTROL

I Procedures

(a) Does the company use statement stickers, and if so how and when?
(b) Are letters used, and if so how and when?
(c) Are letters individually prepared or stereotyped?
(d) Is there a regular letter cycle, and if so how does it work?
(e) Under what conditions does it vary?
(f) How and when is the telephone used?
(g) Which customers qualify for a telephone call?
(h) Is there a regular telephone calling cycle? How does it work?
(i) Under what conditions does it vary?
(j) Who laid down the procedures for telephone calls?
(k) Is a log kept of telephone calls made, and if so what information does it contain?
(l) Is a log of letters kept, and if so what information does it contain?
(m) Are letters sent first-class post?
(n) Are telephone calls timed to take advantage of cheaper rates at different times of the day?
(o) Who prepares letters and signs them?
(p) Who makes telephone calls, and how many per day?
(q) What training has been given to those who use the telephone?
(r) Are personal visits made, and if so by whom?
(s) How often are personal visits made, and to which customers?

II Procedures *Continued*

(a) How is the credit control department advised of receipts and credit note adjustments?
(b) What are the standard credit control documents?
(c) Is there a policy of stopping deliveries to customers, and if so who authorizes it?
(d) What criteria are used as to when and how to apply it?
(e) Who has authority to reinstate deliveries subsequently?
(f) When supplies are stopped, does the company continue supplying goods on a cash on delivery or proforma basis?
(g) Is the customer advised when the stop policy is applied?

III Functions

(a) Who is the credit control department responsible to?
(b) What management reports are produced by credit control? State how often and obtain copies.
(c) Is credit control department responsible for
   (i) Credit ratings?
   (ii) Setting credit limits and re-assessing them?
(d) If credit limits are used, how often are they re-assessed?
(e) Are any of the credit control staff members of the Institute of Credit Management? State who
(f) Does the company belong to a trade association?
(g) If so, is information about mutual customers exchanged within the association (obtain samples)?

(h) What does the credit control department think of its performance in relation to
   (i) The particular industry
   (ii) Industry in general?

IV Collection by third parties

(a) At what state are accounts passed for third party action:
   (i) To debt collectors? Specify which accounts, the average monthly number of accounts and their total value.
   (ii) To solicitors? Specify as above.
(b) What kind of performance is obtained from the various third parties used, and how is it assessed?
   (i) Debt collectors (specify for each)
   (ii) Solicitors
(c) How often do the third parties report back (specify for each one)?
(d) How much does each third party charge?
(e) What is the average cost per pound collected:
   (i) For each debt collector
   (ii) For each solicitor (include legal charges)
(f) What is the average number of accounts passed for legal action each month?
(g) Are there any other accounts of a non-collectable nature which may be distorting the figures (e.g. liquidations, bankruptcies, bad debts)? How many are there, and what is their value?
(h) Why have they not been removed from the ledger?
(i) At what stage are they removed? Are they specially coded? Who authorises their removal?
(j) Does the company have a bad debt reserve? If so, how much, and what criteria is it based on?

V Queries

(a) Give full details of any query handling system
(b) Are queries handled by credit control department?
(c) If not, specify the other departments involved and what type of queries they handle
(d) Does the company produce an analysis of query types? If so, how does it operate?
(e) Are accounts with queries flagged so that no collection calls are made?
(f) Is a query management information report produced?
(g) If so,
  (i) How often?
  (ii) Who does it go to?
  (iii) What information does it show? Obtain copies
(h) Who has authority to place a hold on any credit control activity on an account (e.g. sales staff, credit controller)?

VI Sales/marketing/finance

(a) How strongly is the company oriented towards
  (i) Financial control
  (ii) Marketing
  (iii) Production
(b) Is the prevailing company attitude one of caution?
(c) What is the relationship between the finance and marketing departments?
  (i) Close cooperation
  (ii) Loose cooperation
  (iii) No cooperation/opposition

(d) Does the company ever hold think-tank meetings involving both the marketing and finance departments?
(e) Do they have a policy of one member of a department speaking to other departments about his/her functions? If so, how often, and who attends?

SECTION 7

PERSONNEL

I Staff

(a)
What are the numbers of staff in each of the following categories, and how would you rate their overall calibre?
 (i) Computer operators/data entry staff
 (ii) Ledger clerks
 (iii) Allocation/reconciliation clerks
 (iv) Credit control department
 (v) Middle management
(b) How do you rate the overall feeling of *esprit de corps* within the company?
(c) How do overall pay scales (including overtime, bonuses, holidays and other benefits) rate compared with similar jobs outside the company?
(d) What are career prospects like within the company?
(e) Does it experience staff shortages?
(f) Is recruitment centralized in a personnel department, or do departments take on their own staff?
(g) Who is responsible for
 (i) Advertising vacancies
 (ii) Interviewing candidates
 (iii) Shortlisting candidates

- (iv) Final selection of staff?
- (g) How much use is made of employment agencies to find temporary or permanent staff?
- (h) If problems are experienced in recruiting staff, state which jobs and which departments are affected
- (i) Which departments are currently shorthanded
  - (i) In relation to what the company regards as full strength
  - (ii) In relation to your own estimate of what the company needs?

II The working environment

- (a) Describe the working environment and prevailing atmosphere in each department
- (b) Give details of the equipment and prevailing atmosphere in each department:
  - (i) Desks: are there enough of them, and are they large enough?
  - (ii) Filing systems: where are they, and how is access obtained?
  - (iii) Telephones: how many and where; also whether they are direct lines or on a private branch exchange
  - (iv) Photocopiers: where, how many, and whether they are adequate
  - (v) Microfilming equipment and readers: where, how many, and whether they are adequate
  - (vi) Overall reliability of mechanical equipment

III Senior management

- (a) Is senior management
  - (i) Strong or weak?
  - (ii) Respected or not liked?
  - (iii) Effective or ineffective?
- (b) Is senior management forward thinking?

(c) Are the company's policies, plans, successes and failures communicated adequately to its employees, or does it rely on the grapevine system?
(d) Is there a complaints and suggestions procedure in operation?
(e) Do employees belong to a trades union? Is so, which one? Is there a closed shop?
(f) Is the senior management aware of problems on the shop floor?

SECTION VIII

THE COMPANY IN GENERAL

(a) Are its products or services reliable?
(b) What overall impression did you gain of the company, its management and its attitude to business?
(c) Are its customers content?
(d) Are the various department heads whom you have met aware of any shortcomings
  (i) In their own departments?
  (ii) In other departments?
(e) If so, what are the departments and what are their shortcomings?
(f) Does it appear that anyone is likely to resist or oppose changes for the better; if so, who and why?
(g) Produce a list of everyone met during the review showing
  (i) Those who feel that there is room for improvement in the company
  (ii) Those who do not feel there is room for improvement
  (iii) Those who expressed no opinions
(h) For those who did express opinions either way, what were their specific thoughts?

(i) Were you welcomed and given maximum co-operation?

(j) How many of senior management will be present when you report your findings? Who?

(k) Are there any other factors you have not previously referred to, but consider important in your assessment of the company's needs?